BEARING GOD

The Life and Works of St. Ignatius of Antioch, the God-Bearer

ANDREW STEPHEN DAMICK

ANCIENT FAITH PUBLISHING
CHESTERTON, INDIANA

Bearing God: The Life and Works of St. Ignatius of Antioch, the God-bearer
Copyright ©2017 by Andrew Stephen Damick

All rights reserved. No part of this publication may be reproduced by any means, electronic, mechanical, photocopying, recording, scanning, or otherwise, without the prior written permission of the Publisher.

Published by:
Ancient Faith Publishing
A Division of Ancient Faith Ministries
P.O. Box 748
Chesterton, IN 46304

Unless otherwise noted, Scripture quotations are taken from the New King James Version, © 1979, 1980, 1982 by Thomas Nelson, Inc. Used by permission.

ISBN: 978-1-944967-24-6

Front cover: Wall background, Shutterstock ©inxti
  Roman lion, Depositphoto ©ttatty
Back cover: Colosseum Shutterstock ©givaga

30 29 28 27 26 25 24 23 22 21   16 15 14 13 12 11 10 9 8 7 6 5 4 3 2

*Dedicated to my son
Elias Ignatius
and to
the Church in Syria*

Contents

Preface & Acknowledgments	9
Introduction	15
CHAPTER ONE: Martyrdom	35
CHAPTER TWO: Salvation in Christ	49
CHAPTER THREE: The Bishop	85
CHAPTER FOUR: The Unity of the Church	109
CHAPTER FIVE: The Eucharist	127
Conclusion	153
About the Author	157
Also by Andrew Stephen Damick	159

Since I know you are full of God I have exhorted you briefly. Remember me in your prayers so that I may attain to God, and remember the church in Syria, from which I am not worthy to be called.
(St. Ignatius to the Magnesians 14)

Preface & Acknowledgments

This book took me nearly six years to write. Or perhaps I should say that I wrote the beginnings of it in 2010 and then finished it in 2015–16. It was, in any event, a collection of five short lectures that I originally delivered at St. Paul Antiochian Orthodox Church in Emmaus, Pennsylvania, with the title "Voice from Antioch: An Ignatian Catechism," November 2010 through January 2011. My original purpose for these lectures was to give something of a basic catechism for the Orthodox faith by making use of the letters of St. Ignatius of Antioch, and I am grateful to my flock in Emmaus not only for their attentiveness but also for their interaction. I often thought about these lectures in the years that followed, thinking perhaps I might do something more with them but never quite getting around to it.

I had occasion to think about the lectures quite seriously when I was contacted in October 2014 by my friend Fr. Matthew Howell, an Antiochian priest serving in Wasilla, Alaska. Fr. Matthew had been a seminarian assigned to my parish during the period when I came to Emmaus in 2009. He told me that St. John Antiochian Orthodox Cathedral in Eagle River (a suburb of Anchorage) was interested in inviting me to offer lectures at their annual Eagle River Institute educational event, and he suggested perhaps I might want to dig out my Ignatius lectures.

In my laziness, I always appreciate it when I'm invited to pull out lectures I've delivered before, so I thought this would be nice and easy! But then I discovered that about eight hours worth of lecture and discussion was desired, and I knew my short lectures needed to become a bit longer. My impetus for finally "doing something" with the lectures had come. So I got to work expanding them considerably, adding not only extensive further content to the subject of each of the lectures but also adding more material about the life of St. Ignatius and the history of his letters.

I was particularly pleased to discover the 2013 publication of Gregory Vall's *Learning Christ: Ignatius of Antioch & The Mystery of Redemption*, a scholarly work that is nevertheless quite accessible. Vall does for Ignatius what probably no other patristics scholar has done for him in English—take him seriously as a profound theologian. Vall's scholarship made bringing this book into its current form much easier. I very much recommend reading his work as well, as it is considerably more detailed and expansive than what I am trying to accomplish here. You will notice that Vall is the only modern scholar with whom I interact extensively in this work, which is not intended as a scholarly survey but rather as a popular introduction to Ignatius.

I would not want to leave out, however, the invaluable work of the late Fr. Jack Sparks, whose edition of the *Apostolic Fathers* is the one I used when I first read the Ignatian letters and from which I primarily quote in this book. The translator is Robert M. Grant.

The reader will note that I often use the same quotations from Ignatius in multiple chapters and for different purposes. I did this because so much of what he says yields multiple readings and emphases, and I especially wanted to point out what for me are some of the most memorable passages. For this reason, I've made sure to cite Ignatius thoroughly, and in citations where one of his letters bears the same name as a Pauline letter (i.e., *Romans* and *Ephesians*), I have fully spelled out Ignatius's titles but abbreviated references to Paul's (Rom. and Eph.).

The expanded lectures were delivered August 1–4, 2015, with the title "Voice from Antioch: Key Christian Themes in St. Ignatius the God-bearer," at St. John's in Eagle River, a remarkable community of Orthodox Christians. I was very much blessed by the experience of being with them for those days in Alaska. God has created a wild, stunning country up there, a beauty matched only by their hospitality and love for one another. The parish is led by their capable pastor, Fr. Marc Dunaway, who extended to me the formal invitation to speak there.

I am also grateful for the hospitality in Kodiak, Alaska, prior to my arrival in Eagle River, shown to me by St. Herman's Seminary and by Fr. Innocent Dresdow. Fr. Innocent took me and my old friend Andrew Hall to Spruce Island, among other places. Although the Kodiak folks did not have a direct influence on the writing of this book, my experiences in Alaska will always be bound up with my memories of it. So, for me, they are one.

My gratitude also extends to the "Orthodoxy & Heterodoxy Cabal," a group of Orthodox writers—scholars (both formally and informally trained), theologians, musicians, and clergy—

who not only submit articles for the O&H website but also provide a theological sounding board for each other. I am grateful to them for the helpful comments they provided on my Ignatius lectures and for their friendship and encouragement.

I am also grateful to the folks at Ancient Faith Publishing, who have helped to bring this book to its current state (it's been expanded even further since the Alaska talks), especially to John Maddex. John seems to say "yes" to *almost* everything I suggest, and it somehow turns out well, thanks to his leadership and keen instincts. I sent the beginnings of the new manuscript to him while I was in the process of expanding it for Eagle River with an eye toward publishing it, as I realized that it would be book length by the time I was done. And so, even though I had been planning another book, this one almost by accident jumped the queue and ended up in his mailbox. I am glad that he looked at it and encouraged me to keep sending him the texts.

Thanks also go to author Joel Miller, who helped me settle on the book's title and gave some other helpful suggestions.

I must also thank some people whose names I cannot now remember. Who are they? They are the men and women who, in 1997, when I was first being introduced to Orthodox Christianity largely via the Internet (a context that was much safer and more reliable in those days than it is today), introduced me to the writings of St. Ignatius. Prior to the lengthy exchange of email that I entered upon that summer and fall regarding Orthodoxy, I had not heard of him. So if you happen to be one of those people, thank you. It's partly because of you that I am now an Orthodox Christian.

My special gratitude goes to my wife, Kh. Nicole. Her very practical and hardworking love "in every respect refreshed me in flesh and spirit" (*Magnesians* 12:1). And though at this writing he is only seven years old, this book is dedicated especially to my son Elias Ignatius, who already shows the blessed earnestness of his own patron saints. I hope that someday this book will help him to learn something about one of them.

Finally, this work is dedicated with thanksgiving, love, and prayer to the Christians of Syria, that place where the Godbearer Ignatius labored so long ago, that place that has withstood so much pain and death for two thousand years, bearing witness to the Resurrection of Jesus in martyric life. I have come to know many Syrian and other Middle Eastern Christians in my nearly two decades in the Orthodox Church, and I can attest that the heart of Ignatius still beats in them. I am therefore grateful that my own path led me to be a presbyter of Antioch, that "church in Syria, from which I am not worthy to be called" (*Magnesians* 14).

Fr. Andrew Stephen Damick
Emmaus, Pennsylvania
December 2016

Introduction

WHY I LOVE ST. IGNATIUS OF ANTIOCH

Before we get to the real content of this book on the Hieromartyr Ignatius the God-bearer of Antioch, I wanted to begin by saying something about how I came to be fascinated by this saint, which will in turn lead us to the purpose and method for this book.

Until I was twenty-two years old, I had never heard of St. Ignatius of Antioch. By that point, I had actually heard of precious few saints whose names weren't in the Bible. The name *Ignatius* came into my consciousness in 1997, which was the year that I first heard about something called the Orthodox Church—or, if I had heard of it before, I hadn't spent any time thinking about it. In that year, though, I did start thinking about the Orthodox Church, and that thinking, along with a lot of reading, led me to discover Ignatius of Antioch.

By the time I came upon Ignatius, I had already read about the many differences that Orthodoxy had with the Evangelical Protestantism in which I was raised. The cognitive dissonance that takes place when you read things that take apart your whole religious worldview was firmly in place. I was fast coming to a point where I had to decide either to stop reading about Orthodoxy or to consider making some decisions that would alter the direction of my life. That was the point at which I began reading the letters of Ignatius of Antioch.

Up to that point, what I'd read about the Orthodox Church was largely factual—what the Church believes, what worship looks like, etc. But as I began exploring the letters of Ignatius, I listened to the words of a man who was living this very unfamiliar spiritual life. This was what being a Christian meant for him—he gives a very first-person, very "lived-in" impression. And as I compared what I was reading from Ignatius at the dawn of the second century to what I was reading about the Orthodox Church at the twilight of the twentieth, I realized that they were the same thing. Ignatius was an Orthodox Christian.

As I read, that's when it fully sank in that the kind of Christianity he was describing was truly not my own. It occurred to me that, if this man was actually a member of the New Testament Church itself, actually a direct disciple of the apostles of Jesus, then that meant that, when he described a Christianity that was not like my own, one that in many points contradicted my own, that *he* was right and I was wrong. As a disciple of the Apostles, a first-generation member of the New Testament Church, he had an authority that was not possessed by anyone I had ever met.

Ignatius is the man who made ancient, historic Christianity real for me, and he was also the man who forced me to make a decision about whether I was going to be part of that faith or remain outside it. So it was that I decided to become Orthodox.

I was convinced not by some fast-talking apologist trying to get me to join his church, but rather by the words of a witness to the vitality of the Christian life taught by the apostles, from a time before all the competing schisms, heresies, and denominations that are taken as the norm in our own time.

Over the years that have followed that experience, I've returned to the letters of Ignatius again and again. In their pages, I have many times been reconfirmed in the choice that I made, but I also have found there a fountain of theology, practical wisdom, and encouragement that has watered my own life as a Christian. I have a great affection for this saint, and I even gave my first son "Ignatius" as one of his middle names.

So that leads us to the nature of this present work. I am not a specialist in St. Ignatius, nor am I a patristics scholar. I'm an Orthodox Christian and a pastor, and my appropriation of the writings of this great saint is on those terms. The questions I ask of Ignatius are not just in terms of an apologetic for Orthodoxy's authenticity as the continuation of the early Church but also in terms of what his words mean for us in our spiritual lives in the Church. There is a lot of practical advice there, and there is also some serious theology to shape our knowledge of God so that we, like him, can become "God-bearers." Let's begin with the basic data of who this saint is and what he wrote.

THE LIFE OF ST. IGNATIUS OF ANTIOCH

The great city of Antioch-on-the-Orontes was one of the first places where the Christian Church flourished. In the ancient world, it dominated what was then called *Syria*, which in the

Roman Empire was a much larger region than the modern nation-state by that name. It is now inside modern Turkey and bears the Arabic and Turkish version of the name, *Antakya*. The Antiochian church's foundation was laid by the two chiefs of the apostles, Peter and Paul, and it was Peter who may have acted as the first bishop of that city, the home of the first Gentile church and the home base for many of the apostles' missionary journeys, especially Paul.

Following Peter's episcopacy in Antioch, which may have begun in the year AD 37 and lasted until roughly AD 53, the second bishop for the city was St. Evodius, who served until the year 69. In that year, as reported by the early Church historian Eusebius of Caesarea, Evodius probably died of natural causes, and he was succeeded by Ignatius. (As a side note, Origen claims that Ignatius was the second bishop of Antioch, directly after Peter.)

According to tradition, the first time we hear of Ignatius is found in the *Gospel of Matthew*, in the first few verses of the eighteenth chapter:

> At that time the disciples came to Jesus, saying, "Who then is greatest in the kingdom of heaven?"
>
> Then Jesus called a little child to Him, set him in the midst of them, and said, "Assuredly, I say to you, unless you are converted and become as little children, you will by no means enter the kingdom of heaven. Therefore whoever humbles himself as this little child is the greatest in the kingdom of heaven." (Matt. 18:1–4)

While Matthew does not give the name of this child, there is a tradition that the child is none other than Ignatius, who was likely of Syrian origin. This detail is not mentioned by Ignatius himself, nor does it come up in the text called *The Martyrdom of Ignatius*, which claims to have been written by those who accompanied him on his journey to martyrdom.

The tradition that Ignatius was that child is mentioned by St. Symeon Metaphrastes in the tenth century and Nikephoros Kallistos in the fourteenth. The earliest reference I could track down was in the Matins canon for the saint, written by St. Andrew of Crete, probably in the eighth century. St. Andrew was, no doubt, drawing upon an earlier tradition rather than inventing one.

Depending on how old he was at the point when he may have met Jesus, when Ignatius became the bishop of Antioch in AD 69, he might have been in roughly his mid-thirties or early forties. Prior to his becoming a bishop, along with his friend St. Polycarp, who became the bishop of Smyrna, Ignatius was a disciple of the Apostle John, the writer of the fourth Gospel and the head of the churches of Asia Minor, which was then called Anatolia. The Coptic synaxarion for St. Ignatius says that during his time with John, he traveled with him to many cities. It then says that it was John who ordained him as bishop of Antioch, though other sources say that he was ordained by Peter. Still another says that he was ordained by Paul.

Whatever the case, Ignatius's close association with the apostles and even with the Lord Jesus Himself makes him among the first to receive the message of the Gospel. His youth in comparison with the apostles, about one generation younger, sets him among the second generation of Christian leaders, the first bishops who can truly be called "successors" to the apostles, into whose hands was committed the precious deposit of the life-giving message of Christ.

It is not clear exactly when Ignatius's episcopacy in Antioch came to an end. History records that he was martyred during the reign of the Emperor Trajan. The date Eusebius gives amounts to the eleventh year of Trajan's reign, AD 108. It may have been as early as 98, and some sources put it as late as 117. Whatever the actual date, he was the bishop of Antioch for some decades, perhaps thirty to fifty years. St. John Chrysostom says his rule lasted about forty years. Not much is known about his reign.

One fascinating detail that is known from the time of Ignatius's episcopacy comes from Socrates Scholasticus's *Ecclesiastical History*, which notes that it was Ignatius who introduced antiphonal chanting to the Church. Socrates writes:

> We must now however make some allusion to the origin of this custom in the church of responsive singing. Ignatius third bishop of Antioch in Syria from the apostle Peter, who also had held intercourse with the apostles themselves, saw a vision of angels hymning in alternate chants the Holy Trinity. Accordingly he introduced the mode of singing he had observed in the vision into the Antiochian church; whence it was transmitted by tradition to all the other churches. Such is the account [we have received] in relation to these responsive hymns. (Bk. VI, Ch. VIII)

Music was clearly important to Ignatius, and he uses a musical metaphor in his epistle to the Ephesians (ch. 4). There, the harmonious singing of a choir and the fitting of strings to a harp are likened to the unity of the members of the Church with one another and with the bishop.

During the ninth year of his reign, the Emperor Trajan began a general persecution of Christians throughout the Roman Empire, declaring that they should partake in pagan sacrifices or be killed. Trajan had enjoyed a number of big victories in war, and he believed that it was the pagan gods who had made it all possible. Thus, worshiping them was an act of patriotism for the empire. That's why Trajan singled out Christians for persecution, because their worship of Christ was interpreted as defiance against the empire.

Ignatius's response to Trajan's decree was to preach the Gospel even more fervently than he had already been doing, to urge pagans to become Christians and to give courage to Christians who would not adulterate their faith with the worship of false gods.

Word of Ignatius's defiance of the imperial edict reached the emperor's ears, and the bishop was arrested and brought before Trajan himself while he was sojourning in Antioch for the winter. *The Martyrdom of Ignatius* actually goes so far as to say that it was Ignatius who initiated the arrest, because he was concerned for the Christians of Antioch, that Trajan would begin persecuting all of them. He thus offered himself up so that the emperor would turn his attention away from them.

Sources which describe the final acts of the life of St. Ignatius say that, like the Apostle Paul, before the greatest human power in the world he was dignified and eloquent, courageous in the face of accusations from the head of the empire, and even exultant at the opportunity to bear witness to the Christian faith in such a setting. If you've ever read saints' lives, you know that moments like this can be some of the most remarkable passages in that literature. I'd like to quote here a passage from the traditional account of Ignatius's life, from the section where he confronts Trajan:

> As the two stood face to face, Trajan asked, "Who art thou, thou wretch of a devil, that art so ready to disobey our royal orders, whilst thou seducest others also, that they may come to an equally bad end?" Ignatius answered, "No one who bears God can be called a wretch of a devil. I say this, on the one hand, because the devils stand aloof from the slaves of God; but, on the other hand, if thou sayest this because I am troublesome to the devils, then I concur. For since I have the heavenly King Christ, I confound the devices of the devils." Trajan said, "And who is he that bearest God?" Ignatius answered, "The one who has Christ in his heart." Trajan asked, "Dost thou not think that we too have gods in our hearts, since we have them as allies against our enemies?" Ignatius replied, "Thou art deceived when thou callest the demons of the nations gods. There is one God Who created the heaven and earth and the sea and all things that are therein, and one Christ Jesus, the only-begotten Son of the God and Father, Whose friendship I would be prepared to take risks to enjoy. If thou, O emperor, wouldest come to

acknowledge Him, thou shalt set firm the throne of thy kingdom and wear a splendid diadem on thy brow." Trajan remarked, "Thou speakest, dost thou not, of the One Who was crucified by Pontius Pilate?" Ignatius declared, "I speak of Him Who blotted out the bond written against us and nailed it to the Cross. He put off the principalities and the powers, openly making them an example and triumphing over them in it. He sentenced every malice of the demons to be trampled underfoot by those who carry Jesus in their heart." Trajan then inquired, "Dost thou bear this Jesus in thy heart?" Ignatius answered, "Yea, for it is written: 'I will dwell in them, and walk about with them.'" (*Great Synaxaristes*, December 20, pp. 904–905)

Trajan goes on to offer Ignatius the opportunity to become a high priest of Zeus, if only he would go and render homage to Trajan's gods, making Ignatius first among the emperor's inner circle. He must have seen what a remarkable man stood before him if he would make such an offer to one whom he had made his enemy. Ignatius replies by saying that emperors should only offer favors that would be beneficial to their recipients, and that this "favor" would bring "condemnation and everlasting punishment."

Trajan threatens him with every kind of punishment, but Ignatius says that the very aim and purpose of his life was to go to Christ by a painful death, since the Lord had suffered such things for him. In the face of ridicule by Roman senators standing there with the emperor, Ignatius goes on to preach the Gospel to them all, telling of the Incarnation, death, and

Resurrection of the Son of God, mocking their pagan deities.

The emperor's response was to order him put in chains to be transported to Rome and torn apart by wild beasts as a public spectacle. He did not want him martyred in Antioch because of the honor his flock would show him, supposing that if he were transported a long distance away, Ignatius would die in obscurity. The *Life* says that "with a gladdened heart, he thereupon invested himself with the chains, which he called his spiritual pearls. He also uttered a prayer on behalf of the Church, commending her to the care of God that she might be protected on all sides and preserved until the end in piety. He then followed the soldiers rejoicing."

And so began the great journey to Rome. Some of his Antiochian flock went directly on to Rome ahead of him to be there for his martyrdom.

The elderly Ignatius, who was at least in his late sixties and probably a good bit older, journeyed from Antioch to Rome under a guard of ten soldiers (which he colorfully referred to as "leopards"), sometimes by boat and sometimes by land. Along the way, the guards stopped for an extended rest at the city of Smyrna, which is on the western coast of Anatolia, in what is now the Turkish city of Izmir.

At Smyrna, Ignatius was received with great joy and honor by his friend Polycarp, who was the local bishop, having been appointed there by the apostles themselves. While there, Ignatius, who had become famous for his defiance of the emperor, was visited by delegations from neighboring Christian communities, including Onesimus, the bishop of Ephesus. It is possible that this Onesimus is the runaway slave who was a disciple of the Apostle Paul, who is introduced in Paul's *Epistle to Philemon*. He would be martyred later by stoning.

In Smyrna and everywhere he went, Ignatius was greeted by Christians eager to meet this living martyr, often with great crowds coming to receive his blessing.

During his time in Smyrna, Ignatius wrote four epistles, three to churches in Asia Minor—Ephesus, Magnesia, and Tralles—and one to the Christians of Rome, which particularly urges them not to attempt to intervene with the local authorities to prevent his martyrdom. These letters were likely dictated to a deacon named Burrhus, who was brought by Onesimus.

From Smyrna, he was taken to Troas, on the northwestern edge of Anatolia. There he wrote three more letters, to the churches of Philadelphia and Smyrna, and then the only one written to a particular person, his friend and fellow bishop St. Polycarp. Polycarp later joined him in martyrdom in the year 155, and he is remembered as another of the great figures of second century Christianity. The famed apologist against heresies, St. Irenaeus of Lyons, remembered hearing the preaching of Polycarp in his youth.

In his last letter, the one written to Polycarp, Ignatius says goodbye to his friend with these words: "I bid you farewell always in our God Jesus Christ. May you remain in Him, in unity with God and under His care . . . Farewell in the Lord" (*To Polycarp* 8:3). When Polycarp wrote an epistle of his own to the Philippians, he said of his friend:

> I exhort you all, therefore, to yield obedience to the word of righteousness, and to exercise all patience, such as ye

> have seen set before your eyes, not only in the case of the blessed Ignatius, and Zosimus, and Rufus, but also in others among yourselves, and in Paul himself, and the rest of the Apostles. This do in assurance that all these have not run in vain, but in faith and righteousness, and that they are now in their due place in the presence of the Lord, with Whom they also suffered. For they loved not this present world, but Him Who died for us, and for our sakes was raised again by God from the dead. (*Polycarp to the Philippians*, I:35)

The journey to Rome continued over land, through Macedonia and Illyria, now roughly parts of Greece and Albania, and Ignatius and his captors boarded a boat at the port city of Dyrrhachium, the modern Albanian city of Durrës. From there, they sailed to Neapolis, modern day Napoli (or Naples) in Italy. Upon his arrival in Rome, Ignatius was taken to the Colosseum, the site of numerous martyrdoms of Christians during pagan Roman rule. There, in that most famous of amphitheatres, which could hold up to fifty thousand spectators, the great bishop of Antioch was torn apart by lions, all the while joyfully praising the emperor for the opportunity to be martyred.

Only a very small portion of Ignatius's remains were left after his death, but the faithful were able to obtain the relics and take them back to Antioch for veneration.

After Ignatius yielded up his life for the sake of the One who had yielded up His own for Ignatius, the Emperor Trajan heard the report of how Ignatius had died. The *Life* says that Trajan actually came to revere Ignatius and all Christians, how they were moral people who refrained from shameless acts, how they prayed through the night and were merciful to the suffering. Because they posed no threat to the empire, Trajan felt remorse for his prior treatment and enacted a law that ended persecution of Christians by execution. Ignatius thus went from serving the Christians in Antioch to serving those on the route of his martyrdom to serving all the Christians throughout the Roman Empire. And now his martyric witness, as well as the letters he left behind, inspires all Christians throughout the whole world.

THE LETTERS OF ST. IGNATIUS OF ANTIOCH

Ignatius's letters were prized from the beginning. Ignatius's friend Polycarp, when he wrote a letter to the Philippians, mentioned the letters and their author with honor, saying:

> We are sending you at your request the letters of Ignatius which he sent to us and any others which we possess. They are attached to this letter. You will be able to benefit greatly from them. For they deal with faith and endurance and all the edification which belongs to our Lord. And let us know anything more certain which you learn about Ignatius himself and those with him. (*Philippians* 13:2)

We can see how immediately both the memory of Ignatius and his writings were beloved by the Church.

St. Ignatius's letters were preserved in the churches for many years, but in the fourth century, the collection was tampered with by a forger, who not only added extra material to the authentic letters but actually composed six whole new letters (some late nineteenth-century scholars actually identified eight spurious letters). These all circulated together for a while, but sometime during the Middle Ages, the texts for all of them were lost. Thus it happens that for the majority of Christian history, the authentic writings of St. Ignatius were distorted by spurious additions.

In the fifteenth century, the forged letters were published in a Latin edition, and it is these that are the so-called "Letters of Ignatius" known to some of the Protestant Reformers in the next century. Thus, if you read what the Reformers have to say about Ignatius, it is almost entirely negative. John Calvin, for instance, had this to say while complaining about the observance of Great Lent: "Nothing can be more nauseating, than the absurdities which have been published under the name of Ignatius; and therefore, the conduct of those who provide themselves with such masks for deception is the less entitled to toleration" (*Institutes*, Book I, Ch. 13, Section 29).

The Reformers also tended to reject not only the authenticity of the letters but what was in them. So of course the strong emphasis on the authority of the bishop was seen as "proof" of the inauthenticity of the letters. This rejection, including the judgment that everything bearing Ignatius's name is a fake, actually continues to be accepted in some Protestant circles down to our own day.

Even among those who accept the texts that have through three centuries of scholarship come down to us as authentic, there is still often a rejection of their contents. As an example, a friend of mine in the priesthood, who attended a Protestant seminary before he eventually became Orthodox, told me that the following was publicly asked in a church history course: "In the letters of St. Ignatius of Antioch, you find the full-blown teaching of the magisterial bishop. How did things go so wrong so fast?"

In the seventeenth century, an Anglican archbishop discovered the original letters, setting off controversy as to which were authentic. Various manuscript discoveries have been made in the past few centuries, and so a spirited debate arose. Longer, middle, and short recensions (revised editions of his texts) all were published during this period, using manuscripts from Latin, Greek, and even a long-unknown Arabic version.

Subsequent scholarship, based mainly in examining quotations from Ignatius found in the writings of the Church Fathers, has re-established what is generally regarded as something very closely approximating the original letters in the form we have them today. Through the work of Theodor Zahn and J. B. Lightfoot, it is the middle recensions that have been favored as being closest to the originals. Some people today still reject them all, and the consensus from Zahn and Lightfoot has been challenged several times, but it has mostly been reaffirmed.

As a side note, I think it's important to note that almost everything we now know about Ignatius of Antioch and the actual text of his letters has been established via scholarship in just the past four centuries. Orthodox Christians sometimes are tempted to decry "modern scholarship," especially the historical-critical method, as in itself opposed to the witness of the Holy Fathers.

But what those who say that may not realize is that we actually would not have access to most of what the Fathers wrote without the benefit of the historical-critical method. In fact, throughout most of Church history, the writings of the Fathers were inaccessible to almost every Orthodox Christian—they just weren't available. But now, thanks to the work of scholars—mostly Roman Catholic and Protestant scholars, in fact—there is an enormous amount of material available. And more and more gets published in English all the time.

So while we don't have to accept every conclusion that every scholar comes to, we should give hearty thanks for the long labors of patristics scholars for actually giving us access to the works of the Fathers. Without them, we would have only the spurious and interpolated letters alongside traditional liturgical material about St. Ignatius. The latter is of course quite interesting and valuable, but it is nowhere near the rich bounty of what is actually in his letters.

And what is in those letters is nothing short of magnificent. Roman Catholic patristics scholar Gregory Vall, in his monumental work on Ignatius's letters entitled *Learning Christ* (on which I will often be relying in these pages), makes the argument that the saint's theology in the letters represents a synthesis of elements from the theology of Paul, John, and Matthew (p. 1). Ignatius knew well some of the writings that, centuries later, would be included in the New Testament canon, and he seamlessly incorporated their teachings into his own.

Vall also says in a footnote that the influence of John's theology on Ignatius is profound (p. 1). Yet a close textual reading shows that "evidence of direct literary dependence" is "less than compelling"—that is, it's hard to show that Ignatius was actually familiar with the writings of the Apostle John. But Vall is nevertheless convinced that John deeply influenced Ignatius and says that "it is possible that Ignatius depended on oral tradition rather than on the written Gospel of John." It would make perfect sense if Ignatius were indeed a disciple of John's and knew others of his disciples. The tradition that Ignatius was John's disciple is actually confirmed by the Johannine character of Ignatius's letters precisely *because* he does not quote John. Most of John's corpus was likely composed after Ignatius was already the bishop of Antioch and therefore also after Ignatius's active discipleship under John. That means he probably would not have had access to much of John's writing, if any. Yet the clear Johannine influence on Ignatius's theology strongly suggests actual association with the apostle.

Vall also makes a number of comments about the style and structure of the letters (pp. 52–87), especially with an eye toward criticizing what some scholars have said about Ignatius. For instance, he notes that some scholars have written that these epistles are quite haphazardly composed. One, for instance, said that his letter to the Philadelphians was a kind of "emotional 'outburst'" (p. 57). His letters are also filled with aphorisms, and it is these pithy sayings that are part of what makes them feel so "bumpy" at times.

But Vall takes a close look at the Greek of this letter and notes, by way of example, that Ignatius's summary of his message to the churches of Asia Minor (*Philadelphians* 7:2) was composed "neatly in twenty-eight Greek words, arranged in three rhyming couplets." So Ignatius was literally writing poetry at some points. That is a much more deliberate approach to composition than just rattling off *ad hoc* comments.

Vall also identifies Ignatius as employing "creedal formulae" throughout his letters as part of his signature style (p. 58). By this he does not mean that Ignatius is quoting fixed formulations such as we have in the Nicene Creed, but rather that the structure of a number of passages in the letters is very much like a creed—a series of short statements on various aspects of the Christian faith, usually covering the basic content of salvation history. He notes, "While Ignatius must be drawing on primitive kerygmatic traditions of some sort and obviously intends his creedal formulae to express the church's common faith, it seems that he has handcrafted each of these to serve its particular context" (ibid.). And his creedal formulae often have carefully designed literary structures in them, such as framing devices where similar phrases are used at the beginning and end of the section.

Ignatius can also give mini-homilies in the midst of his letters, another distinctly literary form that indicates how carefully designed his works are (p. 61). In short, Vall gives a thorough and sustained argument that Ignatius is not just giving off-the-cuff remarks in these letters but is very deliberately crafting rhetorically complex and sustained discourses for their recipients.

As a final note on the overall shape of Ignatius's letters, Vall discusses a particularly extreme example of a scholar who does not take the saint very seriously, who accuses him of having authored "slipshod letters that merely give expression to popular piety," saying that he is "more rhetorically persuasive than theologically profound." This scholar, Allen Brent, not only does not take Ignatius's theology seriously but actually criticizes him as an opportunist with an agenda (pp. 79–87).

Now, it might seem pointless to address something like this, but I think it's useful just to take a moment to note that there are people out there who have a radically different view of Ignatius (or any of the Fathers) than is normally seen among Orthodox or other traditional Christians.

Ignatius supposedly was attempting to gain control of the church in Antioch, proclaiming himself as its sole "bishop," and launching a campaign for the new structure of bishop, presbyters, and deacons. He rises up in the midst of chaos in the Antiochian church, where there is a faction that wants a more democratic, purely charismatic style of government and another which focuses on presbyters, who are also apparently at odds with one another. Ignatius is both charismatic and a presbyter, and he tries to commandeer the whole thing to his advantage, leaving the Antiochian church in an uproar. The Romans have to intervene, and so they arrest Ignatius, put him on trial, and sentence him to execution. Ignatius's plan to create the magisterial monoepiscopacy for himself fails.

Vall deals with all this skillfully, but he notes that Brent is not just making this stuff up out of thin air. He is, however, also serving his own theological project (which is what we are doing and what Vall is doing, too). Brent, as we may imagine, is not in favor of bishops. Nevertheless, we can see that interpreting patristic texts can be a complicated affair, and plausible narratives can be designed that may be a bit shocking, even while we disagree with them.

Now that we have said something about both the life and the letters of St. Ignatius, let's begin discussing the aspect of his story that stands out so prominently and about which he has a lot to say—martyrdom.

CHAPTER ONE

Martyrdom

THE SPIRIT OF MARTYRDOM:
"IF ONLY I MAY ATTAIN TO JESUS CHRIST"

One of the things that makes the Christian story so compelling is that people have been willing to die for it. To be sure, people have voluntarily died for a lot of things in history, whether it is because they were fighting for their king, for some cause, or in order to kill or wound other people. But Christian martyrdom is unique. In the historical record, we do not see people dying voluntarily in humility, with joy, and with genuine love for their persecutors the way we see people dying for the Lord Jesus.

Political and ideological martyrdom is almost never voluntary. In fact, when politics or ideology motivate someone so strongly that death comes into play, it's usually by spurring them to violence. Someone who will kill for what he believes in is not motivated in the way a Christian martyr is. A soldier who goes to war may do so because he loves his country, so he risks his life for it, and this is a noble and honorable thing. But true martyrdom is something else entirely.

Yes, there have been other religious martyrdoms in history, but never have they become a kind of core tradition the way they have for the Church. As St. Justin Martyr, a second-century convert from Greek philosophy and martyr himself, once wrote, "Nobody has such great faith in Socrates as to die for his doctrines" (*Second Apology* 10). It is only the one true God who inspires a sustained culture of total and ultimate self-sacrifice. While Judaism had a tradition of martyrdom, such as the Maccabees, it is only with the advent of Christ that selfless, joyful martyrdom becomes a critical element of any religious tradition.

Why? The answer lies with the great mystery and miracle which is at the very heart of the Christian Gospel—the death and Resurrection of Jesus Christ. It is only in Christianity that the martyr joins his suffering and death with that of God, whose death conquers the power of death. The event of Christ's coming and His saving work on the Cross and rising from the tomb have established an entirely new order. Nothing will ever be the same again.

St. Ignatius writes to the Ephesians about this new world when speaking of the virginal conception and birth of Christ:

> Thus all magic was dissolved and every bond of wickedness vanished; ignorance was abolished and the old kingdom was destroyed, since God was becoming manifest in human form for the newness of eternal life; what had been prepared by God had its beginning. Hence everything was shaken together, for the abolition of death was being planned. (*Ephesians* 19:3)

The very character of Christianity is to be martyric. Christianity is the only world religion whose central feature is the martyrdom of its founder. It is the only one where the death and Resurrection of God are the key moment in its narrative. This makes our faith unique, and it also means that martyrdom characterizes who we are as Christians. For Ignatius, the purpose of martyrdom is the very purpose of the Christian life—to attain God.

I have known people who have a great affection for the Orthodox Christian faith or are seriously intrigued by it, but when things get difficult for one reason or another, they fall away. Maybe it gets too hard or too serious or too long, or maybe the cares of this world get in the way, or maybe they just get bored. Maybe it doesn't make sense, or maybe they like their old life too much. Maybe they never believed. Maybe someone disappointed them. Maybe they couldn't see through the human failings of church leaders. Maybe there was a sin they simply could not give up. Whatever it may be, what makes someone stick to the faith and struggle through it, no matter what, is the spirit of martyrdom.

The spirit of martyrdom is critical to being an Orthodox Christian. It is the spirit which of old led even the much-suffering Job to say of God, "Though He slay me, yet will I trust Him" (Job 13:15). It is this spirit that makes Ignatius say, "My desire has been crucified and in me there is no matter-loving fire; there is water living and speaking in me, saying from within me, 'Come to the Father'" (*Romans* 7:2). For Ignatius, that's what martyrdom does for him—it brings him to the Father.

If we are to be true Orthodox Christians, we have to acquire this spirit. It's true that most of us are not gifted with this spirit immediately or completely. But each of us has to come a point when we realize that we would give up everything for Christ in His Church. Then we have to begin living that way, not just saying that we're Christian.

As Ignatius says, "Only pray that I may have power, both within and without, so that I may not only be called a Christian but found to be one. For if I am found to be one, I can also be called one, and then can be faithful when I disappear from the world" (*Romans* 3:2). He would suffer anything for Christ: "Fire and cross, packs of wild beasts, cuttings, rendings, crushing of bones, mangling of limbs, grinding of my whole body, wicked torture of the devil—let them come upon me if only I may attain to Jesus Christ" (*Romans* 5:3). For Ignatius, suffering for Christ was not some special, heroic feat reserved only for super-Christians. It was the normal Christian life, the way of a simple disciple. In his letter to the Ephesians, he writes, "For when you heard that I had been sent in bonds from Syria for our common name and hope, and was hoping by your prayer to attain to fighting wild beasts at Rome—so that by thus attaining I might be able to be a disciple—you hastened to see me" (*Ephesians* 1:2). He says later in this same letter, "now I am beginning to be a disciple" (*Ephesians* 3:1).

When he writes to the Trallians, he even compares miraculous feats with this discipleship and declares being a disciple to be better, saying, "For though I am in bonds and can know heavenly things such as the angelic locations and the archontic conjunctions, visible and invisible, for all that I am not already a disciple" (*Trallians* 5:2). Humility is critical in this life of discipleship—elsewhere, he says, "Then I shall be truly a disciple of Jesus Christ, when the world will not see my body at all" (*Romans* 4:2). He even wants to be completely eaten by the beasts so that he will not leave behind anything to put into a tomb.

Of course, he almost gets his wish—there isn't much left after his martyrdom.

Martyrdom is the normal Christian life, whether it means going to one's literal death or simply dying to the world that we may truly live. Why? Because we share in Christ's own Passion through martyrdom.

THE TRANSFORMATIVE SACRIFICE: "I AM THE WHEAT OF GOD"

When we read the words of Ignatius, especially in his letter to the Romans, we may be struck with how eager he is to face martyrdom. To the modern mind, this is insane. Does it not make more sense to flee the Romans, to fight another day, to continue his ministry? Could he not do more good if he were still alive and serving as the bishop of Antioch, or, if not in Antioch, perhaps somewhere else out of the knowledge or reach of the Romans? How can a violent death be helpful in any way, especially for an old man? Is there something wrong with this man, that he desires death?

Even in a cursory look at Ignatius's *Epistle to the Romans*, which is almost entirely about his impending martyrdom, or the fourteen times in his other epistles he mentions it or his ongoing suffering, we do not see a man who is interested in death for its own sake. There is no nihilistic, morbid fascination with "ending it all." He is not suicidal. Death is not an end for Ignatius, but only the means to an end. It is how he can come to the Father (*Romans* 7:2).

For him, this death which is coming is not death, but the real life. He writes, "Indulge me, brothers: do not keep me from living; do not desire me to die. Do not give the world one who wants to belong to God, nor lead him astray with matter. Let me receive the pure light; when I arrive there I shall be a man" (*Romans* 5:2). If his friends had kept him from martyrdom, that would have meant his real death. They would have been keeping him from real living.

For Ignatius, martyrdom was precisely the path not to death, but to resurrection and freedom. He writes, "I am still a slave. But if I suffer I shall be Christ's freedman and in him I shall rise free" (*Romans* 4:3). He needs to be martyred in order to become free in Christ. Note the irony with which he invests his words about freedom, considering his actual circumstances. He says that his suffering sets him free—and he says this even while in literal chains for Christ's sake. His desire is becoming purified by this suffering, as he says, "Now I am learning in bonds to desire nothing" (*Romans* 4:3).

He also has a clear sense of what he is giving up and how it does not remotely compare with what he stands to gain, saying in another place, "It is better for me to die for Jesus Christ, than to be king over the ends of the earth. I seek him who died for us; I want him who rose for us" (*Romans* 6:1). Perhaps in this we might hear a little of a rebuke toward the emperor himself—

Ignatius prefers to die for Jesus rather "than to be king over the ends of the earth," a title which basically describes what Trajan was. He wants Jesus Christ, who died and rose for us, far more than imperial authority.

In another passage, he compares his departure from the world with the setting sun: "forming a chorus in love you may sing to the Father in Christ Jesus that God has judged the bishop of Syria worthy to be found at the west after sending him across from the east. It is good to set from the world toward God so that I may rise toward him" (*Romans* 2:2). If his life's sun sets in this world, it will rise toward God.

Because Ignatius so connects his impending death with the Resurrection of Christ, for him death cannot be the end. It is rather a beginning, and not just a beginning, but transformation. This transformation comes about in terms of sacrifice: "Grant me nothing more than to be poured forth to God while an altar is still ready" (*Romans* 2:2). This is his chance. He does not want anyone to get in his way, because such an "altar" might not be ready another time. He says later, "Pray to Christ for me that through these means I may be found a sacrifice to God" (*Romans* 3:2).

Perhaps his most famous saying comes from this same letter to the Romans, where he not only describes his martyrdom in terms of sacrifice, but as a sacrifice that will transform him into someone acceptable to Christ: "Let me be food for the wild beasts, through which I can attain to God. I am the wheat of God and I am ground by the teeth of wild beasts so that I may be found the pure bread of Christ" (*Romans* 4:1).

As Gregory Vall points out (p. 146), there is the basic

sense here that a thing often needs to be destroyed, or "disintegrated," so that it can serve a higher purpose. Food is digested for nourishment, trees are ground up for paper, and so forth. The image here is of wheat that is ground to become flour for bread. Of course, the flour-mill here is the teeth of the wild beasts.

This is also a clear allusion to the Eucharist—as we will discuss in the sixth chapter, Ignatius's martyrdom in some sense transforms him into the Eucharist. Through his suffering, he is becoming the sacrifice of the altar.

We hear an echo of the words of the Apostle Paul, who wrote in his own epistle to the Romans, "I beseech you therefore, brethren, by the mercies of God, that you present your bodies a living sacrifice, holy, acceptable to God, *which is* your reasonable service" (Rom. 12:1). Ignatius is fulfilling the admonition of the apostle.

REVEALING CHRIST: "I AM A WORD OF GOD"

For Ignatius, martyrdom is not only normal but is a sacrifice that transforms the Christian to be acceptable to God, a true man, an enlightened, changed, perfected, resurrected person. At the same time, Ignatius regards his martyrdom as a witness of Christ to the world.

His *Epistle to the Romans* dwells almost exclusively on the theme of his martyrdom, because he fears that the Christians in Rome, some of whom were probably Antiochian Christians who had run on ahead of him, may try to intervene with the imperial government to spare him.

As such, most of the letter is spent persuading them that his martyrdom is better than his release. He therefore urges them to be silent and not to interfere, precisely so that he can become an even greater witness—the literal meaning of *martyr*—than he could if he continued in the earthly life. He writes, "For if you are silent about me, I am a word of God; but if you love my flesh, I shall again be only a voice" (*Romans* 2:1). How prophetic he was, for the voice of this martyred bishop now rings across the millennia to us, preaching to us not just as one voice, but as "a word of God."

In becoming "a word of God," Ignatius understands his sufferings as revealing Christ's true nature as the God-man. One of his major pastoral concerns throughout his epistles is in fighting against a heresy which had sprung up known as docetism, which taught that Christ only appeared to be a man and that His suffering and death were only apparent and not real. They had no problem with the idea that He was God; they just didn't believe that He was a real man. Orthodox doctrine makes a big difference for Ignatius, and he recognizes that heretical doctrine means a different kind of Christian life. Ignatius refers to the docetists in his letter to the Smyrnaeans as "beasts in human form, whom you must not only not receive but, if possible, not even meet—but only pray for them, if somehow they may repent. This is difficult, but Jesus Christ, our true life, has power over it" (*Smyrnaeans* 4:1).

But if what the docetists say is true, then what is the point of the suffering and death of Christian martyrs?

Ignatius writes to the Trallians about this. Much of this passage has the "creedal formula" sound that Vall mentions:

> Be deaf, then, when anyone speaks to you apart from Jesus Christ, who was of the family of David, who was of Mary, who was truly born, ate and drank, was truly persecuted under Pontius Pilate, was truly crucified and died, while heavenly, earthly and subterranean beings looked on. He was also truly raised from the dead, when his Father raised him up, as in similar fashion his Father will raise up in Christ Jesus us who believe in him—without whom we have no true life. But if, as some godless men—that is, unbelievers—say, his suffering was only apparent (they are the "apparent" ones!), why am I in bonds, why do I pray to fight wild beasts? Then I die in vain. Then I lie about the Lord. (*Trallians* 9:1–10:1)

His belief in the Resurrection is so powerful, and he identifies the reality of Christ's humanity as so central to the Christian faith, that Ignatius finds it unthinkable, a "lie about the Lord," that anyone should submit to suffering and death if Jesus' humanity weren't real. Ignatius's martyrdom proclaims the humanity of Christ—something which was much more a subject of debate in his time than the Lord's divinity. There would be no point to his martyrdom if the Son of God had not truly become a human man and truly suffered. The reason why Christian martyrdom joins us to Christ is because Christ's Passion was real. He sees no point in the suffering of the martyrs if Jesus is not truly both God and man, saying, "For if these things were done by our Lord only in appearance, I too am in bonds in appearance. Why have I given myself up to death, to fire, to the sword, to beasts?" (*Smyrnaeans* 4:2).

These sufferings are not in vain—"But near the sword is near God, with the beasts is with God. Only in the name of Jesus Christ I am enduring all things in order to suffer with him; and the perfect man himself empowers me" (ibid.). To suffer for Christ is to become one with Him, and because He is the "perfect man," He can empower other men to suffer, to die, and to rise again.

Martyrdom is therefore not only one "witness" among many but is the Christian witness *par excellence* (Vall, p. 157). This is because, more than any other kind of Christian witness, it is a joining to the true sufferings of the God-man Jesus Christ. That people suffer and die for Christ is the most perfect witness to the Lord's own suffering and death.

This suffering is revelatory both for the Christian and for the world that puts him to death. Vall writes:

> Any time Christians live out the gospel with anything approaching authenticity, some tension between Christianity and the world will be apparent. But when Christians live out the gospel so radically that the world can no longer tolerate their presence, the true identities of both world and church are manifest. When the world singles out individuals and groups of Christians for persecution and execution, the true nature of the conflict and the identity of the participants involved are revealed. (p. 157)

Martyrdom reveals who the Christian is and what is the true nature of the world that kills him. And because Christians are called to be "God-bearers," martyrdom therefore reveals the Christ in whom the Christian finds his hope.

Christian martyrdom not only changes the one who undergoes it, but it also proclaims the true doctrine about Christ. Likewise, the properly lived Christian life will preach Christ to all those around, whether words are used or not. If a Christian lives martyrically, giving up his earthly desires and becoming dead to the world, his life will be marked by resurrection. Even if that resurrection will not be complete until the age to come, even earthly existence can become a lifelong homily, a revelation of the true identity of Jesus Christ.

"ALSO CALLED THEOPHORUS"

In the opening greeting of all his letters, St. Ignatius refers to himself by another name, *Theophorus*, which means "the God-bearer." It's interesting that he calls himself this rather than using the title of *bishop*. It's not clear exactly how he got this name, but it may refer to that encounter with Jesus when he was a young child. In that case, *Theophorus* may also mean "borne by God," because Jesus took him into his arms. In a real sense, though, from his life we can see that he was not only carried by God but that he carried God within himself. Vall says that this term is part of Ignatius's claim that he is speaking on behalf of God (p. 328).

If he truly carried God within himself, then he was the bearer of immortality. It made sense for him to go to martyrdom, because it was the seal of his Christianity. Martyrdom for Ignatius was the ultimate proof that he carried the Resurrection of Christ within himself. That he had been chosen—not by the Emperor Trajan, as it seemed to the world, but by God—to be offered up as a sacrifice, to become united mystically to that sacrifice of the Eucharist he himself had offered up for decades in Antioch, is why Ignatius is so joyfully assured of his salvation.

It is not as if dying itself guarantees anything. But Ignatius's knowledge of God's presence within him, that he was the God-bearer, made it so that when he was finally confronted by the emperor, martyrdom was the perfect climax to his story. Of course it should be that a man who carried God within himself should in his life and death imitate the One who was the God-man.

The life, martyrdom, and writings of the God-bearer Ignatius have truly become for us "a word of God," a clear message to us across the many centuries of Church life, coming to us almost from the very beginning of the Gospel's introduction to the world. From the world's perspective, Ignatius must seem like a crazy failure, a man who had a successful position and then gave it all up because he wouldn't compromise. He could have finished out a successful career with prestige and honor if only he had done as the emperor asked—even more, he could have risen higher than he had ever dreamed, for the emperor offered him a place in his own inner circle.

But like all the words that God speaks to us, this martyr provokes us into examining ourselves and our priorities more closely. Ignatius reveals that Christian life is about the kind of commitment that seeks out Christ no matter the cost, even if it is earthly life itself. He also shows us that living our lives as sacrifices for God, putting our desires last and truly suffering for the faith, is the only context in which we can be transformed into real men and women, real disciples, holy and acceptable to God, filled with divine light. And in living that life which only comes from Christ, the "perfect man" who can empower us, we proclaim His perfect God-manhood to the world.

May we be challenged and inspired by this magnificent figure from the earliest years of the Church to become like him, "God-bearers" who carry the divine presence into the world.

CHAPTER TWO

Salvation in Christ

We saw in the previous chapter how St. Ignatius of Antioch laid great stress on his martyrdom, that for him it was not a rare characteristic of Christian life but its culmination, sharing in Christ's Passion and death in the fullest sense. Martyrdom for Ignatius is a "given" in the Christian life. It is the precondition on which everything else is based. If the Christian is not willing to give up his whole life to Christ, then he is not a Christian. In this chapter, we will discuss what comes next. What does it look like when someone is willing to give his life over to Christ? What does it mean to be saved? What is the Christian's identity?

CHRISTIAN IDENTITY

It may seem odd in our modern world to ask this question of identity, since we tend to see people primarily in terms of their function in society. One of the first questions we routinely ask of someone we've just met is what they do for a living. What is your function? How do you fit into the Great Machine?

And these days, while it is not usually polite to ask about this at first, we also often identify people according to their desires. It may be as innocuous as, "What are you into?" That is, "What are your hobbies, interests, etc.?"

But we also now define people by their emotional desires, especially in terms of sexuality, and most particularly if that sexuality is not the "standard" type that God created at humanity's beginning. Someone who is "straight" is less likely to see that as key to his identity as someone who identifies as "gay," "queer," "transsexual," etc.

There are also various tribes of identity politics that one may consider even apart from the kind pushed by the sexual revolution. We identify people by race, color, ideology, social class, and so forth.

But the question that has concerned Christians from the beginning of the revelation of Christ has not been about function, desire, or various tribes of culture and color. It is about the identity of Jesus Christ and how we conform to Him. We recall how in Mark 8, the Lord Jesus asks His disciples, "Who do men say that I am?" They put forward several rumors they've heard—he must be John the Baptist, Elias, or one of the prophets, back from the dead. Then He asks, "Who do you say that I am?" And Peter answers him with power, "You are the Christ" (Mark 8:27–29).

Jesus, in the great High Priestly Prayer for His disciples that He prays before His Passion, says, "And this is eternal life, that they may know You, the only true God, and Jesus Christ whom You have sent" (John 17:3). Knowing the Father and knowing Him for who He is are exactly the terms in which Jesus Himself defines what it means to have eternal life, what it means to be saved. This knowledge is not only important for the Christian, it is the very essence of Christianity. Without it, we are not Christians but only people following some "religion."

We should never get tired of asking who God is and who we as Christians truly are. We should especially never get tired of asking how we can narrow the identity gap between us and God.

Knowing who Jesus is and who we are in relation to Him has been the focus of Christianity from the beginning. How different this approach is from what normally passes for Christian life in our day, which is so focused on various activities, programs, and organizations that questions about authentic Christian identity are so often lost.

I'm sure that we all know people who would probably regard themselves as "good Christians" who nevertheless might stare at you blankly if you asked them who Christ is and what they were doing to become conformed to His identity.

But this is what Christianity is about, as we will hear from the voice of Ignatius the God-bearer, who lived in the very shadow of the Lord Himself. Ignatius has a lot to say about conforming his identity to the identity of Jesus Christ.

A CHALLENGE TO CHRISTIAN IDENTITY: THE JUDAIZERS

We tend to think of Christianity in our own day as a discrete religious faith, but in the time of Ignatius, there was still the living memory of Christians having been expelled from the synagogues. There were also people alive in his time who remembered going to the synagogues and the temple in Jerusalem with the apostles. The first Christians were all Jews, and they regarded the revelation of Christ as being the fulfillment of the Law of Moses. It only made sense that they would in many ways continue practicing as Jews.

Yet with the destruction of the temple in AD 70 and the growing estrangement of the followers of Christ from the followers of the rabbis, not to mention the rapidly increasing population of Gentile converts into the Church, the successors to the apostles, the bishops, saw a greater need to define themselves as distinct from Judaism.

Yet there were Christians who saw this distinction as having gone too far, and we see the beginnings of a debate about this question even in the New Testament. It seemed to have been settled at the Apostolic Council in Jerusalem (Acts 15), which ruled that it was not necessary for Gentiles to be circumcised—that is, to become Jews—before they could be Christians. But in Ignatius's time, there nevertheless remained Judaizers, Christians who taught that the Church was not remaining Jewish enough. It's not clear from his letters which Judaizing practices were being promoted. Ignatius speaks about the Judaizers in his epistles to the Magnesians and the Philadelphians.

Ignatius's attitude to these people was to show them how Judaism was not above Christ, but Christ above Judaism, and not only that, but that Judaism is fulfilled in Christ. In his epistle to the Magnesians, he writes, "Do not be deceived by strange doctrines or by antiquated myths, since they are useless. For if we are still living in conformity with Judaism, we acknowledge that we have not received grace" (*Magnesians* 8:1).

This echoes the sentiments of Paul, who also fought against Judaizers, and who declared that whoever claimed to be justified by the Law was fallen from grace (Gal. 5:4). It also echoes the words of John the Baptist, who says in the first chapter of the Apostle John's Gospel that "the law was given through Moses, *but* grace and truth came through Jesus Christ" (John 1:17). If we are following Judaism after the advent of the Son of God, then we do not have the grace of Jesus Christ.

Ignatius doesn't always use strong contrasts as he addresses Judaism and Christianity. Sometimes, he instead reads the Old Testament in clearly Christian terms. For Ignatius, the Old Testament is about Jesus.

He even goes so far as to claim the Old Testament prophets not for the Israel of the Old Covenant, but for the Church, the New Israel of the New Covenant, writing,

> For the most divine prophets lived in conformity with Christ Jesus. For this reason they were persecuted, though inspired by his grace to convince the disobedient that there is one God who manifested himself through Jesus Christ his Son, who is his Word which proceeded from silence and in every respect pleased him who sent him. (*Magnesians* 8:2)

Ignatius not only sees Christ foretold in the Old Testament, but he says that the true meaning of the lives of the prophets is found only in Christ. This approach to the Old Testament

Scriptures was also used by many of the Church Fathers, who sometimes even went so far as to tell the Jews that those Scriptures did not belong to them but to the Church.

For Ignatius, setting aside the Sabbath and instead participating in Christian worship is the true path to following the prophets:

> If, then, those who lived in antiquated customs came to newness of hope, no longer keeping the Sabbath but living in accordance with the Lord's [day]—on which also our life arose through him and his death (though some deny it), and by this mystery we received the power to believe, and for this reason we endure so that we may be recognized as disciples of Jesus Christ, our only teacher—shall we be able to live apart from him of whom even the prophets were disciples in the Spirit, him whom they expected as their teacher? And therefore when he came, he whom they righteously awaited raised them from the dead. (*Magnesians* 9:1–2)

Not only is the Lord's Day (that is, Sunday) the proper day for worship, but the prophets were Jesus' disciples "in the Spirit" and were awaiting resurrection from Him.

In his letter to the Philadelphians, where a division had arisen over the question of how Christianity related to Judaism, Ignatius affirms the value of the Jewish prophets, claiming them for the Church, even speaking of them almost as if they were apostles of Jesus:

> The prophets we also love because they made a proclamation related to the gospel and set their hope on him and were waiting for him; by believing in him they were saved, being united with Jesus Christ. Worthy of love and admiration, they are saints, attested by Jesus Christ and numbered together with us in the gospel of the common hope. (*Philadelphians* 5:2)

With this kind of language, Ignatius engages in a recapitulation of the Old Covenant in terms of the New Covenant of Jesus Christ. The prophets themselves become Christians. He has no problem claiming them for the Church. He even goes so far as to say that the way to the Father whom the Jews worship is Jesus Christ:

> The priests are noble, but the High Priest, entrusted with the Holy of Holies, is nobler; he alone has been entrusted with the secrets of God; he himself is the door to the Father, through which enter Abraham and Isaac and Jacob, and the prophets and the apostles and the Church. All these are in the unity of God. But the gospel has something distinctive: the coming of the Savior, our Lord Jesus Christ, his passion and resurrection. For the beloved prophets made a proclamation related to him; but the gospel is the perfection of imperishability. (*Philadelphians* 9:1–2a)

The message of the prophets of Judaism was good because it was ultimately about Jesus, but it was as yet imperfect. The Gospel of Jesus has perfected that message. Note again the "creedal" material here—a summary of the life of Jesus, mentioning His coming, His Passion, and His Resurrection. This is the Gospel which is "the perfection of imperishability." This is the direct line from Abraham to the Church, with Jesus at the center (Vall, p. 60).

Note also his deft use of the imagery of the priesthood of the Old Covenant: these priests are "noble," but the High Priest—that is, Christ—is "nobler." Using the figure of the Holy of Holies—the most sacred part of the Jewish temple—Ignatius says that Jesus is the "door to the Father" that everyone from Abraham to the apostles and the Church enters through. It's a beautiful image.

Ignatius does not satisfy himself, however, with trying to convince his readers that the Old Testament prophets were really followers of Christ. He still wants to make clear that Judaism's time is over and Christianity's time has begun. He also knows that some will not believe him, and so he exhorts those who are willing to listen:

> But if anyone interprets Judaism to you, do not listen to him. For it is better to hear Christianity from a man who has received circumcision than Judaism from one who has not. Both of them, if they do not speak of Jesus Christ, are tombstones to me and graves of the dead on which nothing but human names are inscribed. (*Philadelphians* 6:1)

He also says that there is no need to be called by any name other than the name *Christian*. Ignatius knows that names mean things and help to impart identity to those who use them, so he insists that Christians not think of themselves as Jews but only as Christians:

> Whoever is called by any name other than this does not belong to God. Therefore put aside the bad leaven, now antiquated and sour, and turn to the new leaven, which is Jesus Christ. Be salted with him, so that none of you may be spoiled, since you will be tested by your odor. (*Magnesians* 10:1b–2)

It's interesting to note that here and elsewhere he talks about Judaism as being "antiquated," while also affirming the value of the prophets. But Judaism is not the "bad leaven" by virtue of being inherently bad, but rather it has "spoiled" because its time has passed. Christ, the "new leaven," has now come.

He still lays claim to Judaism's foundations and says that its power actually comes from Christ, writing, "It is absurd to talk about Jesus Christ and practice Judaism. For Christianity did not base its faith on Judaism, but Judaism on Christianity, in which 'every language' believing in God was 'brought together'" (*Magnesians* 10:3).

Shocking as that kind of language might seem in our own time, this kind of sentiment is expressed by other Fathers of the Church. And why should it not be so? After all, if Jesus Christ really is the incarnate Son of God, the One who created the world and revealed God to Abraham, Isaac, Jacob, and Moses, then why should we not read the Old Testament in the light of the full story now revealed?

In what is perhaps his clearest recapitulation of Jewish tradition in terms of the revelation of Jesus Christ, Ignatius addresses the problem in Philadelphia, where the Judaizers were appealing to the Old Testament as their final authority. If they could not find a given Christian teaching borne witness to in the "archives" of those texts, they would not believe it. This view had caused the division in Philadelphia, what Ignatius here calls "factiousness":

> I exhort you to do nothing out of factiousness but according to the learning of Christ. For I have heard some say, "If I do not find it in the archives [that is, the Old Testament], I do not believe it in the gospel." And when I said to them, "It is written there," they answered me, "That is the question." But to me Jesus Christ is the archives. The inviolable archives are his cross, death and resurrection, and the faith that comes through him. It is by these, through your prayers, that I wish to be justified. (*Philadelphians* 8:2, Vall translation, p. 28)

Again, Ignatius redirects the authority for Christians back toward Jesus Christ Himself, the One to whom the Scriptures, including the Old Testament, bear witness.

Even though he has negative things to say about Judaism, probably the furthest Ignatius goes in that negativity is to say that Judaism's time had passed. But his overall approach to Judaism is not to deny the authenticity and authority of the Old Testament Scriptures but rather to include them in the Christian Gospel. Their true meaning, he argues, is found in Jesus Christ. What was begun with the Old Covenant is completed in the New.

A CHALLENGE TO CHRIST'S IDENTITY: THE DOCETISTS

Another challenge to early Christian identity took the form of a challenge to Christ's own identity as the God-man, a challenge that would be made again and again over the next several centuries of Church life. The particular challenge Ignatius battled was docetism, the teaching that Jesus was certainly God but only *appeared* to be a man. (The word *docetist* comes from a Greek word meaning "it seems" or "it appears.") We saw in the previous chapter how Ignatius vociferously rejected this teaching, saying that, if true, it would make his martyrdom utterly pointless. If God did not become a man who truly suffered in the flesh, then what was the point of the men who followed Him suffering in their own flesh?

Some Ignatian scholars have suggested that Ignatius is really addressing a single heresy in his letters—a kind of docetic Judaism (or gnostic Judaism), but most seem to agree these days that he really is addressing two. At the very least, there is clearly a distinction in his texts—while his letters to the Magnesians and Philadelphians address the Judaizers, the docetists come under criticism in his letters to the Smyrnaeans and Trallians. Those who defend the "two-heresy view" point out that the two heresies are inherently incompatible. Vall writes, "Docetism denies the true humanity of Christ and can lead to a nonhistorical view of redemption, while Judaization sees Christ as merely one in a long historical sequence of inspired prophets and teachers." Ignatius's theology is therefore an attempt to steer between these two heretical temptations (Vall, pp. 69–70).

Docetism is referenced again and again in Ignatius's writings, and its beginnings are found even in the writings of the New Testament. The Apostle John mentions the docetists in his first general epistle, in the fourth chapter:

> Beloved, do not believe every spirit, but test the spirits, whether they are of God; because many false prophets have gone out into the world. By this you know the Spirit of God: Every spirit that confesses that Jesus Christ has come in the flesh is of God, and every spirit that does not confess that Jesus Christ has come in the flesh is not of God. And this is the *spirit* of the Antichrist, which you have heard was coming, and is now already in the world. (I John 4:1–3)

Is it any wonder that Ignatius, who was John's disciple, should also speak of these heretics so forcefully? This was clearly a problem in the early days of the Church.

In the first part of his epistle to the Smyrnaean Christians, in his greeting to them, Ignatius writes a kind of short creed regarding Christian faith, which is meant to refute the heresy of the docetists:

> I give glory to Jesus Christ, the God who made you so wise; for I know that you are established in immovable faith, as if you were nailed in flesh and spirit to the cross of the Lord Jesus Christ and confirmed in love by the blood of Christ—being convinced concerning our Lord that he is truly of the family of David as to the flesh, Son of God by God's will and power, truly born of a virgin, baptized

by John so that "all righteousness" might be "fulfilled" by him, truly nailed for us in the flesh under Pontius Pilate and the tetrarch Herod. (*Smyrnaeans* 1:1–2a).

One can almost hear the beginnings of the Nicene Creed in his words, more than two hundred years before it would be ratified at the First Ecumenical Council. Note that he has no problem here referring to Jesus Christ as "the God who made you so wise." There is no question that He is God, and Ignatius does not go on at length about that but rather insists on the truth of Christ's humanity, His birth, His Baptism, and His death on the Cross. The story of the life of Jesus is critical to Ignatius's understanding of Christianity.

Christology is always expressed also as soteriology. Ignatius emphasizes the humanity of Christ as "fleshly," writing in that passage that Christ is "truly nailed for us in the flesh," yet he also writes that Christians are "nailed in flesh and spirit to the cross." Thus, while he emphasizes that our own crucifixion in the spiritual life encompasses the whole human person—flesh and spirit—his emphasis on Christ's Crucifixion focuses on the flesh that made that Crucifixion possible. Crucifixion for us can be understood as a metaphor, but we cannot make it a metaphor for Christ. His true flesh was truly nailed on the Cross.

Wrapped up in Christ's identity is the story of His life. Ignatius tells us clearly that the reality of Christ's suffering, death, and Resurrection are critical to salvation itself: "For he suffered all this for us so that we might be saved, and he truly suffered just as he truly raised himself—not, as some unbelievers say, that he appeared to suffer" (*Smyrnaeans* 2:1a).

Note that he here clearly makes a claim for Christ's divinity, saying that it was He who raised Himself, something only God can do. In the teachings of the Apostles Peter and Paul, the language they use is that God (or sometimes "the Father") raised Jesus from the dead (Acts 2:24, 32; 3:15; 4:10; 13:30; Rom. 10:9; 1 Cor. 15:15; Gal. 1:1; Col. 2:12; 1 Thess. 1:10; 1 Pet. 1:21).

But in John's Gospel, we see Christ claiming that He will raise Himself (John 2:19–22). If we recall that Ignatius was John's disciple, it makes sense that he uses his language. There is of course no contradiction here, since the power to raise the dead is the power of the Holy Trinity, shared by the Father, Son, and Holy Spirit. So we can at once say that God raised Him, that the Father raised Him, and that He raised Himself, all without contradiction.

John's Gospel is also written later than the Pauline and Petrine teachings and represents a theological refinement of the Christian message. As such, while the foremost among the apostles may have been initially hesitant to refer to Jesus raising Himself from the dead, the Apostle John, who is most explicit in stating directly that Jesus is God in a number of passages, writes that Jesus raised Himself from the dead.

In the spirit of his teacher John, Ignatius also goes so far as to call those who do not believe in Christ's true humanity "unbelievers." They're not some "alternative" kind of Christians, they're *unbelievers*. He also says of these people, some of whom may have been admirers of his, "How does anyone help me if he praises me but blasphemes my Lord and does not acknowledge that he is clothed in the flesh? He who says this has absolutely denied him and is clothed with a corpse" (*Smyrnaeans* 5:2).

The English phrase "clothed in the flesh" here is one word in Greek: *sarkophoros*, literally "flesh-bearing." Then he calls those who deny Christ's coming in the flesh *nekrophoros*, meaning "corpse-bearing" or "death-bearing." You cannot have life in Christ if Christ does not have true human flesh. Ignatius has no qualms about using some pretty graphic imagery to illustrate his point. He even says to the Ephesians that heretical teaching gives off a stench like a decaying corpse (*Ephesians* 17:1).

There's no possibility for compromise here, because there are only two ways to live. He writes to the Magnesians:

> Since, then, actions have a consequence and two goals lie before us, death and life, and each is going to go to his own place; for just as there are two coinages, the one of God, the other of the world, and each has its own stamp impressed on it, unbelievers that of this world, believers (with love) the stamp of God the Father through Jesus Christ; and unless we voluntarily choose to die in relation to his passion, his life is not in us. (*Magnesians* 5:1–2)

For Ignatius, people who do not believe in Christ's true suffering and participate in it are not Christians, because they deny the mystery of who Christ is. Further, Ignatius sees the oppositions between life and death or between good and evil as *both* characterizing the *physical* world of humanity. The material realm is not only the realm of death and evil but also that of life and goodness. Christ's suffering in the flesh is thus also a refutation of the docetic view of the universe, which identifies evil with the material flesh and goodness with the immaterial spirit.

Marveling at this mystery, Ignatius writes what appears to be a poem or hymn about Jesus Christ in his letter to the Ephesians: "There is one Physician: / both flesh and spirit, / begotten and unbegotten, / in man, God, / in death, true life, / both from Mary and from God, / first passible and then impassible, / Jesus Christ our Lord" (*Ephesians* 7:2).

This explodes the docetic view of Christ as merely appearing to be a man in multiple ways. Most obviously, He is "both flesh and spirit." But He is also "begotten and unbegotten," that is, having a beginning from His mother but "unbegotten" from before all time (He does not mean here to speak on the Son's eternal origin in the Father). He is "in man, God," "in death, true life." Both those phrases would drive a docetist crazy—how can God be in man or life be in death? The docetic universe does not allow for materiality to bear divinity and life. He is "both from Mary and from God," having both human nature and divine nature, which makes Him "first passible and then impassible." *Passible* is a word meaning that something can be acted upon. He is "first passible" not because His human nature is "first" but because His humanity is how we first perceive Him. He is "impassible" because He is God. And, as Ignatius began emphasizing the "one Physician," he completes this passage by naming Him as "Jesus Christ our Lord."

If you look at the structure of this passage from Ignatius, you will see that it follows a chiastic shape—that is, poetically, its phrases, which proceed thematically forward in the first four and then in the reverse order thematically in the second four, may therefore be arranged in the form of the Greek letter *chi*

(X), which is an ancient symbol of Christ (because it is the first letter of *Christos*, the Greek word for "Christ"):

(A) There is one Physician:
(B) both flesh and spirit,
(C) begotten and unbegotten,
(D) in man, God,
(D) in death, true life,
(C) both from Mary and from God,
(B) first passible and then impassible,
(A) Jesus Christ our Lord.

CHRISTIAN IDENTITY AS MYSTICAL UNION WITH CHRIST

Even aside from his words against the docetists, Ignatius has a lot of other things to say about who Jesus Christ is. In his letter to the Ephesians, he says that Christ is "our inseparable life" and "the mind-set of the Father" (*Ephesians* 3:2b; the latter phrase here is Vall's translation, p. 350). That is, the Father's purpose for us and for the world is that we might be joined to Him, that our life might not be separated from His, because if it is, then we are dying and not living.

This union of the Church with Christ is so intimate as to be comparable to the union of the Son with the Father. When he exhorts the Ephesians to be unified with their bishop, he writes, "How much more blessed do I consider you who are mingled with him as the Church is with Jesus Christ and as Jesus Christ is with the Father, so that all things are harmonious in unison!" (*Ephesians* 5:1).

This comparison of the union of the Church amongst its members with the union of the Father and Son is precisely an echo John's theology, expressed in John 17:21, where Jesus prays for the unity of the Church not only in terms of being between its human members but in terms of His own unity with the Father. And the unity the disciples manifest reveals Jesus' mission from the Father.

Ignatius makes the point that it is only within the Church that this union with Christ is possible, putting it in eucharistic terms: "Let no one deceive himself: unless a man is within the sanctuary, he lacks the bread of God. If the prayer of one or two has such power, how much more does that of the bishop and the whole church?" (*Ephesians* 5:2). Clearly, something powerful and mystical is happening within the Church, such that there is great power for salvation. The wholeness of the Church is needed for this powerful prayer that brings a man into the sanctuary where he can access the bread of God.

He says later to the Ephesians, "Therefore be eager to meet more frequently for thanksgiving [*eucharistian*] and glory to God. For when you frequently come together, the powers of Satan are destroyed and his destructive force is annihilated by the concord of your faith" (*Ephesians* 13:1). I can think of no better exhortation to frequent participation in church services. Still further, though, this "concord of your faith" or "the unanimity of faith" (Vall translation, p. 165) that annihilates the destructive force of Satan is manifested in the mystical union with Christ that takes places in the context of the eucharistic synaxis of the believers with their bishop.

The word translated here as "concord" or "unanimity" is *omonoia*, which literally means "the same mind." Ignatius certainly means here the union of believers with each other found in worship, but it is not only a mysterious union but a true union in doctrine, which is necessary for the eucharistic synaxis in which union with Christ happens.

Ignatius says to the Ephesians that by this means they become "companions on the way, God-bearers and shrine-bearers, Christ-bearers, bearers of holy things, in every respect adorned with the commandments of Jesus Christ" (*Ephesians* 9:2a). This language must have been especially powerful for Ignatius—he gives the Ephesians his own nickname.

The "commandments of Jesus Christ" which can adorn us "in every respect" enable us not only to learn *about* Christ or *from* Christ but to learn the very person of Christ (Vall, p. 257). That is why we can become "Christ-bearers." We bear Jesus Christ in us by being adorned with His commandments.

For Ignatius, Christian life is not about having a right status with God (as would become an important theme in Reformation theology) but about bearing God within ourselves. It is about communion with Him and with each other, a communion so intense and intimate that we can be said to be "bearers" of God, of Christ, of holy things, that we become "shrine[s]" or "temples."

The word which is translated here as "shrine-bearers" is *naophoroi* and can also be translated "temple-bearers." We become bearers of the *naos*, which literally means "ship," but which is used in the Christian tradition to refer to the church building. *Naos* is the origin of our English word *nave*, which refers to the main worship space in a church. For Ignatius, we can become churches, the very place where God is met and worshiped.

One verse earlier, Ignatius introduces this image of the Ephesian Christians as places of worship: "You are stones of the Father's temple, made ready for the edifice of God the Father, raised to the heights by the crane—the cross—of Jesus Christ, and using the Holy Spirit for a rope. Your faith is your upward guide and love is the way that leads up toward God" (*Ephesians* 9:1b).

When Vall translates this passage (p. 114), he translates the word for "rope" instead as "cable," which makes the engineering image a bit clearer. Thus, we get Christians as temple stones for the edifice of the Father, being lifted up by the crane which is the Cross of Jesus, using the Holy Spirit for the cable. And the motion of this machine building the temple of the Father, stone by stone, is guided by the faith and love that lead up toward God.

All this is possible only because of the true humanity of Christ, which Ignatius stresses again and again in his criticisms of the docetists. He therefore links Christ's bodily humanity even after the Resurrection with salvation itself, writing:

> And when he came to those with Peter he said to them, "Take, handle me, and see that I am not an incorporeal demon." And they immediately touched him and believed, being mingled with his flesh and spirit. Therefore they despised death and were found to be above death. (*Smyrnaeans* 3:2)

For Ignatius, we are saved not from a bad standing before God (a common idea today, an inheritance from the Reformation), but from death itself. Their mingling "with his flesh and spirit" are what enable them to "despise death" and to be "found to be above death." Contrary to what the docetists would say, Christ's true humanity is what allows us to be "mingled" with Him. Because Christ enables our conquest of death, a new order is coming into the world, an order which shakes the world to its foundations and destroys the old order. When Ignatius writes about the new order that has been ushered in by the coming of Christ, he says that

> the old kingdom was destroyed, since God was becoming manifest in human form for the newness of eternal life; what had been prepared by God had its beginning. Hence everything was shaken together, for the abolition of death was being planned. (*Ephesians* 19:3b)

And how was "the abolition of death" being planned? It was through the revelation of God in Christ, God in human flesh.

While writers dealing with later doctrinal controversies among Christians would argue about salvation primarily in legal terms, Ignatius's approach is much more primal, more immediate, and echoes more firmly the language of the Bible itself. When Paul writes to the Hebrews about the priesthood of Christ and why He came to the earth, he says,

> Inasmuch then as the children have partaken of flesh and blood, He Himself likewise shared in the same, that through death He might destroy him who had the power of death, that is, the devil, and release those who through fear of death were all their lifetime subject to bondage. (Heb. 2:14–15)

In the Orthodox Christian faith, salvation is primarily about winning the battle against death and the devil. As the passage from Hebrews indicates, the bondage which those in the power of Satan experience is expressed primarily as the fear of death. Fearing death, man in bondage tends to do everything he can to make his own life comfortable and secure, even at the expense of others.

Only in this light is Ignatius's joy at his own martyrdom properly understood. He was not going so joyfully to his death in Rome because of, in the words of Fr. John Romanides, some psychosis or "eschatological enthusiasm" (that is, trying to hasten the end of the world), but rather his joy is "the consequence of the realization of the inseparable relationship existing between death and Satan." Fleeing martyrdom "would have meant slavery to Satan" (*The Ecclesiology of St. Ignatius of Antioch*, section 1). It is because of the freedom found only in Christ's abolition of death that Ignatius is so ready for martyrdom, that he is practically running toward it. Since participation in Christ means being above death, what is granted instead is incorruptibility. It is this gift of incorruptibility that is bound up in the very identity of Christ. The Hebrew *Messiah* and the Greek *Christos* both mean "anointed one," and so it is to the very meaning of Jesus' mission on Earth that Ignatius refers when he writes, "The Lord received anointment on his head for this reason—that he might breathe imperishability upon the Church. Do not be anointed with the evil odor of the prince of this age, lest he take you captive from the life set before you" (*Ephesians* 17:1).

Note here that eternal life is a goal "set before you," but the devil can "take you captive" from it. Salvation is not a guarantee.

You have to keep following Christ. You have to stay faithful. The choice is clear: follow Christ, and He will "breathe imperishability" on you. You will be immune from death, having become imperishable. Receive instead the anointing of Satan, "the evil odor of the prince of this age," and he will put you into slavery, snatching you away from the life that is set before you.

IDENTITY AND THE CHRISTIAN LIFE

Having heard Ignatius's voice on who the Christian is to be, how he is to be freed from the "antiquated" ways of Judaism, how he is to profess the true humanity of Christ, how he is to be closely united to Christ, receiving incorruptibility from Him, we should also ask ourselves what kind of advice Ignatius has for the day-to-day life of the Christian. What does this salvation look like? In what way does the Christian live that sets him apart from the rest of the world?

Once again, the question of identity is key to Ignatius's teaching on the proper Christian life. He writes, "Men of flesh cannot act spiritually, nor can spiritual men act in a fleshly way, just as faith cannot perform deeds of unfaith or unfaith those of faith" (*Ephesians* 8:2a). Who you are will determine what you do. You have to be united to Christ, to be a spiritual, faithful person, in order to be able to behave spiritually and faithfully. The proper Christian life comes from being a proper Christian.

This is backwards from those who believe that the Christian life consists merely in performing certain actions, especially moral actions, that what you believe does not really matter. But such acts, if performed by people out of obligation, for personal gain, or even just from a dedication to morality rather than out of faith, are really "the deeds of unfaith" and not those of faith.

Ignatius goes on to say that, if someone is truly spiritual, then even the things that he does "according to the flesh" are also spiritual (*Ephesians* 8:2b). He is not only refuting the gnosticism of the docetists here but also saying something about who we are as Christians—if we have true faith, then everything that we do becomes a spiritual act. Nothing is mundane.

There is no sharp separation in Ignatius between the fleshly and the spiritual. But it is the spiritual which is to rule us, and that makes even our fleshly acts spiritual. Why? He says it is because "You do everything in Jesus Christ" (*Ephesians* 8:2b). Because Christ is a divine person with a deified humanity, as we share in His humanity what we do becomes spiritual.

When we turn to God and pursue union with Him we will become spiritual men and women, people of faith who naturally do the deeds of faith. When we become those people, all of life takes on a different character. No longer are our spirits darkened and subjugated to the whims of our bodies, but our bodies become obedient to our illumined spirits.

A consistent Christian life is proof of faith:

> No one who professes faith sins, nor after obtaining love does he hate. The tree is manifest from its fruits. So those who profess to belong to Christ will be recognized by what they do. For a deed is not a matter of professing now but of continuing to the end by the power of faith. (*Ephesians* 14:2)

Christian life is therefore not just a matter of doing some good deeds here and there, of "supporting" your church, etc., but of "continuing to the end by the power of faith." Once again, the faith in your heart is what makes your profession of faith and the deeds that follow it have reality. And that faith gives you "power" to endure to the end.

Ignatius insists that it is who you are that matters most. What you do will naturally follow. This insistence is entirely consistent with the message of Christianity throughout the ages, which has concerned itself with the heart and its union with God. The motivation must come from within.

Ignatius allows two possible sources of motivation: "We should either fear the wrath to come or love the grace which is present, one of the two, just so that we may be found in Christ Jesus for true life" (*Ephesians* 11:1).

It is better to be motivated by love for God than out of fear of the wrath to come, but sometimes it is only out of a genuine knowledge of the consequences of sin—"the wrath to come"—that we come to our senses and return to God, so that we can be "found in Christ Jesus for true life."

This word "found" here refers to our eschatological hope, a hope Ignatius mentions often. Because a day will come when this present life will come to an end and the age to come will finally begin, and whatever spiritual place we are "found" in then will be our eternal destiny from then on. That is why Ignatius so often speaks of wanting to be "found" in Christ or Christ's disciples as being "found to be above death" (*Smyrnaeans* 3:2). The "finding" is how Christ will find us when He returns to Earth in His glory, and it indicates an objective character to the judgment of God (Vall, pp. 191–192).

But his concern is not only for what is coming at the end of time. Ignatius speaks of loving "the grace which is present." God is not out there somewhere. His grace is present with us. In Orthodox theology, we most often speak of grace as being uncreated—that is, grace is the presence of God Himself. So it makes sense that Ignatius would say that we can "love the grace which is present"—that is, we can love God.

Note also another contrast here—the wrath is to come, but grace is present. God continues in His patience and mercy to withhold the future wrath that will eventually be visited upon those who have broken His covenant, and He gives grace right now so that we can experience the effects of salvation.

Once the proper relationship of the spirit to the body is established—that the spirit rules the body, not the reverse—then all of life becomes spiritual. There is no spiritual "part" of life. There is only life, which is spiritual. As Ignatius writes, "But what you do in relation to the flesh is spiritual, for you do everything in Jesus Christ" (*Ephesians* 8:2b).

This vision is decidedly different from those who try to inject the secularized vision of compartmentalization even into church life. Some people believe that there are "spiritual" parts of life in the parish and "business" parts, and they try to arrange authority and responsibility accordingly. The division that exists in their own lives, where some things are "spiritual" but other things are otherwise, is being projected onto the very Church of God.

This approach to church life is sometimes called the "upstairs/downstairs church." That is, the "spiritual" part, governed by the clergy, happens "upstairs" in the church. Everything else, governed by the lay leadership, happens "downstairs" in the parish social hall. The laity don't tell the clergy how to run the church services, and the clergy don't tell the laity how to spend the money.

But such a division is alien to Ignatius. The Christian is always a God-bearer, whether he is serving the Divine Liturgy or scrubbing toilets, and so he is subject to the authority and ways of the Kingdom of God, not those of secular society. It is contradictory to suggest that there can be any "secular" side to either a Christian or his parish community, because God is always there with us. Ignatius says:

> Nothing escapes the Father's notice; even our secrets are near him. We should therefore do everything on the assumption that he dwells in us, so that we may be his temples and he may be our God in us—as is the case, and as will be manifest before our face by the effects of the love which we justly bear toward him. (*Ephesians* 15:3)

If we are temples where God dwells, everything that we are and everything we do is spiritual. If, as Ignatius says, we are God-bearers, there can be no secular life for the Christian.

There can also be no "upstairs/downstairs church." All that is to be done can only be done as prayer, under the spiritual leadership of the bishop and his appointed representative. It is not that clergy are qualified to do everything—they need the expertise and experience of everyone in the parish. It is that all—including the laity—are ministers in the church, and the bishop or his presbyter is the chief minister, the one who directs all.

Every ethical teaching or act ultimately is referred back to the Lord Jesus, which is why Ignatius gives this kind of advice to his friend Polycarp, especially focusing on marital purity:

> Flee from evil arts, or indeed preach sermons about them. Tell my sisters to love the Lord and to be content with their husbands, both in flesh and in spirit. Similarly, in the name of Jesus Christ command my brothers to love their wives as the Lord loves the Church. If anyone is able to remain in purity, in honor of the Lord's flesh, he must do so without boasting. If he boasts he is lost, and if it is made known to anyone but the bishop, he has been corrupted. It is fitting for men and women who marry to be united with the bishop's consent, so that the marriage may be related to the Lord, not to lust. Everything is to be done in God's honor. (*To Polycarp* 5:1–2)

This advice is ostensibly about marriage, but it continues his theme that everything must "be related to the Lord." And because that is true, there is nothing here about marrying or staying married to fulfill one's own desires, which are unpredictable and unreliable. That is why the marital union has to be "with the bishop's consent"—otherwise, instead of being "related to the Lord," it is related "to lust."

And what does it look like when the marriage is "related to the Lord"? Married women will "love the Lord" and "be content with their husbands, both in flesh and spirit." It is sometimes easier to be content with someone in his flesh but not his spirit, or perhaps the other way around. But Ignatius wants wives to be content with both. And he tells husbands "to love their wives as the Lord loves the Church." This echoes St. Paul in the New Testament (Eph. 5:25). How does the Lord love the Church? He died for her and gave Himself up for her.

Ignatius therefore urges wives to be content and husbands to be self-sacrificial. As a good pastor, he knows what kinds of temptations men and women have, and so he gives advice appropriate to each. Women tend to be discontented, and men tend to be selfish. So wives and husbands have their work in the marriage laid out for them, so that everything can be "related to the Lord" and "not to lust."

All must be "in God's honor," which is perfect and trustworthy. Note especially here that even if someone chooses a life of abstinence for God's sake—remaining "in purity, in honor of the Lord's flesh"—he has to do it without making a show of it, telling it only to his bishop (who, in Ignatius's time, is his local pastor). If he goes around bragging about it, "he is lost," and "he has been corrupted." Because we carry God around with us wherever we go, the only possible life that Christians can live is one of humility, even in the face of those who attack us. When speaking about those who have departed from the true faith and how Christians ought to be toward them, Ignatius writes,

> And you must pray unceasingly for the others—for in them is hope for repentance—that they may attain to God. Therefore let them be instructed by you, at least by your deeds. With their wrath you be mild, with their

> boastful speech you be humble-minded, with their abuse you offer prayers, with their deceit you be firm in faith, with their cruelty you be gentle, not eager to imitate them. (*Ephesians* 10:1–2)

Why should we behave thus toward our enemies? "In them is hope for repentance—that they may attain to God." There is hope for everyone. That can be hard to remember at times, but we should desire with Ignatius that even our enemies "may attain to God." And then they will no longer be our enemies but brothers and sisters in the Lord. We can even give them instruction by our deeds, he says, by being mild with their wrath and humble-minded with their boasting, by offering prayers for their abuse, firmness in faith for their deceit, and gentleness for their cruelty. Is this not the way of Christ?

This approach to confronting heresy and all the evils of this world is precisely the one the Lord Himself took, which is why Ignatius continues:

> Let us be found their brothers in our forbearance; let us be eager to be imitators of the Lord, to see who can be the most wronged, defrauded, rejected—so that no plan of the devil may be found among you but that in complete purity and self-control you may remain in Jesus Christ, in flesh and spirit. (*Ephesians* 10:3)

The Lord became our brother even while we were ungodly and sinners. We should imitate Him and "be found their brothers in our forbearance," even accepting unjust abuse just as He did. In this way we "remain in Jesus Christ, in flesh and spirit."

Such humility does not, of course, require quietism, that we never speak the truth boldly—just look at the life of Ignatius himself! But how different this vision of humility is from the world's vision, which teaches us to stand up for our "rights" and never to accept being unjustly harmed. Ignatius speaks differently. To the Smyrnaeans he writes, "Office must puff no one up, for faith and love are everything and nothing is preferable to them" (*Smyrnaeans* 6:1b). Ignatius often links faith with love, and one who has both cannot be puffed up by his "office" or anything else. Nothing is preferable to them, and the one who has them is humble.

But this is martyrdom! And martyrdom makes no sense to the world: "My spirit is devoted to the cross, which is a stumbling block to unbelievers but salvation and eternal life to us. 'Where is the wise man? Where is the debater? Where is the boasting of the so-called intelligent?'" (*Ephesians* 18:1, see 1 Cor. 1:20). The courage of Ignatius, found in his spirit's devotion to the cross, is what makes possible his humility, a humility that brings him even to martyrdom. The cross is "a stumbling block to unbelievers but salvation and eternal life to us."

"I KNOW YOUR FERVOR FOR THE TRUTH"

At the end of his letter to his friend St. Polycarp, Ignatius includes a short address to the flock there at Smyrna which his friend shepherds. In it, he gives a summary of the Christian life as advice to the Christians under Polycarp's care, painting a beautiful, vigorous image of what the Church can be like if all things are done according to God's desires. He writes:

> Pay attention to the bishop so that God will pay attention to you. I am devoted to those who are subject to the bishop, presbyters, and deacons; and may it turn out for me that I have a portion with them in God. Labor together with one another, strive together, run together, suffer together, rest together, rise up together—as God's stewards and assistants and servants. Be pleasing to him for whom you are soldiers, him from whom you will receive your pay. None of you must be a deserter. Let your baptism serve as a shield, faith as a helmet, love as a spear, endurance as full armor. Your works are your deposits so that you may receive the full sum due you. Therefore be patient with one another in gentleness, as God is with you. May I always have joy in you. (*To Polycarp* 6:1–2)

As Ignatius so often does, he exhorts that attention be given to those who lead the Church. If we pay attention to the bishop, then we have God's attention. We invoke God's care by sticking with the bishop and following him. We do not make a solitary appeal to God apart from the bishop's leadership. Ignatius is devoted to those who are subject to the clergy. Why? It is so that he may "have a portion with them in God." He is not devoted to the obedient for the sake of the pride of the clergy—as we read earlier, "office must puff no one up." No, his devotion is because this is the order that God has ordained, and if we follow it attentively, then we can have that "portion with them in

God." He sees his own salvation as being with those who hold obedience to the clergy.

What is the spirit with which we are to be obedient? "Labor together with one another, strive together, run together, suffer together, rest together, rise up together—as God's stewards and assistants and servants." He tells us what obedience looks like, and we do these things together in unity because we serve together in the household of God.

He then changes to a military image, calling us soldiers who are paid by the Lord and are armored by Him. This is not quite the same way that Paul describes the "armor of God" in Ephesians 6, but it's the same basic image. I must admit that I love the idea that baptism serves as a shield.

Then Ignatius uses a monetary image: "Your works are your deposits so that you may receive the full sum due you." This metaphor is especially helpful when we may think of the good that we do as being useless when we don't see immediate results. We should not expect immediate results from our "deposits" of good works. The "full sum due" us is our salvation, not earthly success.

And then this: "Therefore be patient with one another in gentleness, as God is with you." This is difficult, isn't it? But if we remember that God is patient and gentle with us, then perhaps it can be easier for us to do the same for someone else. We are responding to God's patience and imitating Him in His gentleness by giving that to others.

Then finally, "May I always have joy in you."

Not only does Ignatius give Polycarp's flock those vivid, beautiful exhortations, but he again returns to his theme of union and co-labor with God, who gives all the strength needed to do everything, writing this:

> A Christian has no authority of his own but spends his time for God. This is God's work, and yours as well when you complete it, for I am confident that by grace you are ready to do the good deed appropriate to God. Since I know your fervor for the truth, I exhort you with only a few lines. (*To Polycarp* 7:3)

God's work becomes our work: "This is God's work, and yours as well when you complete it, for I am confident that by grace you are ready to do the good deed appropriate to God." A sharp division between God's work and the work of Christians is nowhere to be found in the writings of this disciple of the Apostle John. Rather, we see here a synergistic view—God and man working together.

For Ignatius, if we are united to God, then His work becomes our work. What other work is there than the salvation of mankind? What else can there be for the Christian than becoming mystically one with God in Jesus Christ? That is why we can receive the "full sum" due us, not because God owes us anything for our works, but because we have become co-workers with Christ (1 Cor. 3:9), because our works are the work of God. What we receive is God Himself, who is our salvation, because we have been doing God's works.

Let's close out this chapter with the final line from that passage: "Since I know your fervor for the truth, I exhort you with only a few lines." How would you like to hear a martyr say that to you? Is that not the kind of encouragement that we need?

I know your fervor for the truth. I must admit that I hear in these words an echo of the encouragement written down by Ignatius's teacher the beloved Apostle John from his apocalyptic vision of Jesus Christ, written to these same Smyrnaean Christians. Here is what He said to them:

> And to the angel of the church in Smyrna write, "These things says the First and the Last, who was dead, and came to life: 'I know your works, tribulation, and poverty (but you are rich); and *I know* the blasphemy of those who say they are Jews and are not, but *are* a synagogue of Satan. Do not fear any of those things which you are about to suffer. Indeed, the devil is about to throw *some* of you into prison, that you may be tested, and you will have tribulation ten days. Be faithful until death, and I will give you the crown of life.'" (Rev. 2:8–10)

I know your works.

Perhaps we could summarize the teaching of St. Ignatius on what it means to live the life in Christ with those final words: "Be faithful until death, and I will give you the crown of life."

CHAPTER THREE

The Bishop

Perhaps no theme has been more explored by scholars and theologians in the writings of St. Ignatius than the episcopacy. Books, papers, articles, theses, and dissertations have all treated this topic, penned in many cases by some truly great minds, so we cannot presume in any sense to make an exhaustive study of it in this chapter. Nevertheless, we will try to give an overview of Ignatius's teachings on the episcopacy with a fresh look at his epistles.

Because of his antiquity and closeness to the apostles, Ignatius's legacy is one that all Christians interested in the early Church must come to terms with. As a church leader, he is a direct successor to the apostles in the most literal sense, as well as being a disciple of John, one of the inner circle of Jesus along with Peter and James. This makes him an authoritative witness to what the apostles taught and how the Church functioned.

Roman Catholics love and venerate Ignatius and include him on their calendar of saints. Yet he may be challenging for them, as there is nothing in the writings of this early saint to support the claims to supremacy for the pope of Rome. Ignatius offers nothing for that ecclesiology, even when writing to the church in Rome.

Ignatius is perhaps more striking and more challenging for Protestants, most of whom do not have bishops, or, if they do, they are primarily administrative officers and not seen as successors to the apostles. Ignatius, who stands in the shadow of the apostles themselves, presents such a robust and forceful image of the episcopacy that he challenges those who regard bishops as some later medieval accretion. Indeed, so striking is his language that the nineteenth century saw various Protestant scholars attempting to disprove the authenticity of any text bearing Ignatius's name. Ironically, it was through this scholarly work that their genuine character was finally established.

For the Orthodox tradition, Ignatius presents neither a challenge nor a problem, because his teaching on the episcopacy is essentially what we still teach and practice (that does not mean that we do not sometimes fail to live up to our own teachings). In his writings, we see the bishop as he ought to be for us even now. He is still the leader of worship, the focus of Church unity, and an integral part of the local church body, the one to whom obedience is due—the icon of God Himself. Perhaps the only significant difference is that the bishop is no longer the local pastor for most congregations, as he was for Ignatius.

"ONE WHO HAS . . . CHRIST AS HIS BISHOP"

The overarching image of the bishop found in Ignatius's letters is spoken perhaps most poetically and clearly in the salutation with which he begins his letter to his friend Polycarp. In that letter, he salutes "Polycarp, bishop of the church of the Smyrnaeans (or rather, one who has God the Father and the Lord Jesus Christ as his bishop)" (*To Polycarp*, Salutation). Literally, he is "overseen (*episkopimenos*) by God the Father and the Lord Jesus Christ" (Vall translation, p. 346). For Ignatius, the bishop, while a towering figure in the Church, is nonetheless a servant, one who has God as his bishop. Christ is the head not only of the Church catholic—for God is the "bishop of all" (*Magnesians* 3:1)—but He is also the bishop of the bishop in particular. The bishop therefore lifts all men up, because he himself is lifted up by the Lord (*To Polycarp* 1:2).

The bishop is indeed at the center of his church; however, he is not there as a tyrannical and absolute ruler, but as one who is truly the servant of all. If Ignatius is so strenuous in his insistence that the bishop must be obeyed, it is not because he preaches order for its own sake, but rather he preaches the grace that God has given to the bishop. Believers are to follow their bishop and give him obedience, but it is in the same vein as the Apostle Paul urges the Christians of Corinth: "Imitate me, just as I also *imitate* Christ" (1 Cor. 11:1).

Further, there is no antithetical relationship here between the bishop as an institutional office and the charismatic leadership granted by God. Ignatius sees the two as closely connected. The episcopacy is both an office and a charismatic gift from God. The gift requires the office in order to be stable, and the office requires the gift in order to be efficacious. For instance, when Ignatius speaks to the Ephesians about their concern for their bishop Onesimus as being insufficiently graced by God, he speaks of Onesimus as "a man of inexpressible love"

(*Ephesians* 1:3). God is "blessed" "who gave you the gift (*charisamenos*), worthy as you are, of obtaining such a bishop" (ibid.). The bishop is therefore a charismatic gift from God, "graced" to the community (Vall, p. 346).

The bishop's authenticity is also expressed by preaching the word of God correctly, warding off heresy (something mentioned repeatedly by Ignatius), and having "God's mind-set" (*To Polycarp* 4:1, Vall translation). There is an objective character to the faith and the "mind-set" that the bishop must have in order to be functioning correctly. He must "speak truly of Jesus Christ," and no one should listen to anyone who does not (*Ephesians* 6:2). Doctrine and morality are specific and set, not a matter of private opinion.

Vall writes, "Effective episcopal authority is a three-legged stool, combining office, charism, and what is elsewhere called 'the standard of truth' [Irenaeus of Lyons, *Adv. Haer.* 1:9:4] or 'the standard of our tradition' [Clement of Rome, *1 Clem.* 7:2]" (p. 347). One could say exactly the same thing of the presbyterate, for parish priests, whose authority derives from the bishop, need to function in all the same ways.

PRESIDENT OF THE SYNAXIS: "WHEREVER THE BISHOP APPEARS"

One of Ignatius's most famous sayings is found in his epistle to the Smyrnaeans: "Wherever the bishop appears, the whole congregation is to be present" (*Smyrnaeans* 8:2). This is sometimes shortened to the slogan, "Where the bishop is, there is the church."

The bishop is properly the bishop when he presides at the Eucharist. Of the many things that Ignatius has to say about the clergy in general and the bishop in particular, he always comes back to the same locus for the clerical ministry—the altar in the midst of the gathering of the believers. This coming together for worship—the synaxis—is what the Church is. It is precisely a worshiping community.

When Ignatius says to the Smyrnaeans, "Apart from the bishop no one is to do anything pertaining to the church," a firm statement of the bishop's authority, the very next sentence is, "A valid Eucharist is to be defined as one celebrated by the bishop or by a representative of his" (*Smyrnaeans* 8:1b). That which is "pertaining to the church" is worship. The Church's whole purpose is worship, and therefore the bishop's purpose is worship. Leading worship is not a sideshow for an otherwise purely administrative office. It is the whole point of the office.

The English word *bishop* is derived directly from the Greek *episkopos*, which means "overseer." And what does the bishop oversee? He oversees corporate prayer, most especially the celebration of the Eucharist. Ignatius therefore urges his friend and fellow bishop Polycarp to have more church services, writing, "Meetings should be more frequent; seek out all individually" (*To Polycarp* 4:2). It is the duty of the bishop to connect with each member of the congregation and to bring him into meeting for worship. The bishop is not just the one who presides at the synaxis but also the one who convenes it.

Christians have to answer the bishop's call, and when they are at one with him in worship, they are purified: "He who is within the sanctuary is pure; he who is outside the sanctuary is not pure—that is, whoever does anything apart from the bishop and the presbytery and the deacons is not pure in conscience" (*Trallians* 7:2).

All of the mysteries of the Church find their touchstone in the grace given by God to the bishop: "It is not right either to baptize or to celebrate the agape apart from the bishop; but whatever he approves is also pleasing to God—so that everything you do may be secure and valid" (*Smyrnaeans* 8:2b). The "agape" spoken of here is most likely the Eucharist, though some scholars translate *agape* as "love feast," a communal meal in the early Church that may have been connected with the Eucharist. In either case, these central worship acts of the local church gathered together are to be considered "secure and valid" only with the bishop at the center. While these passages define the bishop, they also define the Church's sacraments. Neither baptism nor the Eucharist can be performed without the bishop. According to Ignatius, these are not simply ordinances (outward expressions of obedience and faith without inherent effects) that may be performed by just anyone. They can be done only by the bishop or "by a representative of his." We see here that while the worship of the Church is performed by the whole assembly, it is only complete and secure if the one ordained to lead it is doing so.

We also see here an indication that the Eucharist may be celebrated by a delegate of the bishop, probably a presbyter (though he does not say so explicitly). We must remember that in Ignatius's time, the bishop was the head of the local congregation. It is only later that multiple parishes served by presbyters begin to be formed within one local church with the bishop at the head. But we see in Ignatius's letters the possibility for this development.

Yet even as the practice of the Church develops to make the bishop's representative at the Eucharist (rather than the bishop himself) the most common occurrence, the norm for worship is still the bishop's presidency, as seen most fully in the hierarchical liturgy. The presbyter only ever serves with the blessing of his bishop. He never has the "right" to serve of his own accord. Yet the bishop, so long as he remains in the Orthodox faith, in communion with the Church and in a relationship of love with his fellow bishops, needs no one else's blessing.

In the need for the clergy to have the bishop's blessing to administer the holy mysteries of the Church, we see how this authority works. Without these sacraments, there is no Church. Therefore, without the blessing of the bishop, the local church does not function. At the same time, lest we think that the bishop has this authority of himself, Ignatius tells Polycarp, "Nothing is to be done without your approval, and you must do nothing without God—as indeed is your practice; stand firm" (*To Polycarp* 4:1b). The bishop's authority is derived from outside himself.

He also writes to the Philadelphians, "I know that your bishop obtained his ministry, related to the whole community, 'not from himself or through men' or for vainglory, but in the love of God the Father and the Lord Jesus Christ" (*Philadelphians* 1:1a). Thus, the bishop's sacramental office is revealed as belonging ultimately to God and His love for the Church—he is not self-ordained, and his office does not come from earthly politics.

If the presbyters, deacons, and laity cannot worship without the bishop, neither can the bishop worship without God. The sacramental authority the bishop has is the authority God has given to the Church, and Ignatius says that the clergy were ordained by "Jesus Christ, who established them, in accordance with his own will, in security by his Holy Spirit" (*Philadelphians*, Salutation).

The power of this authority and the great effect that it can have are expressed potently when Ignatius writes to the Ephesians, "If the prayer of one or two has such power, how much more does that of the bishop and the whole church?" (*Ephesians* 5:2b). It is not the bishop's prayer alone that has this power, nor is it only the "whole church" that can pray like this—it is the prayer of the church being led by the bishop. This is neither autocracy nor democracy, but true hierarchy—an order that has its source and leadership in the sacramental high priesthood.

This order and hierarchy of worship finds its fulfillment in unity. It therefore permits only a single bishop and a single celebration of the Eucharist, precisely because there is one Christ. He writes to the Philadelphians, "Be eager, therefore, to use one Eucharist—for there is one flesh of our Lord Jesus Christ and one cup for union with his blood, one sanctuary, as there is one bishop, together with the presbytery and the deacons my fellow slaves—so that, whatever you do, you do it in relation to God" (*Philadelphians* 4).

THE LOCUS OF UNITY: "I SAW YOUR WHOLE CONGREGATION"

As we mentioned earlier, the modern Roman Catholic vision of Church unity being defined by subjection to a worldwide bishop in Rome is not found in Ignatius's writings. We saw how he described his friend Polycarp, the bishop of Smyrna, as "one who has God the Father and the Lord Jesus Christ as his bishop." He does not say that Polycarp has the bishop of Rome for his bishop nor even a regional Asian primate (i.e., a senior bishop in his area). Since he himself is a bishop, Polycarp's bishop is God.

With all that Ignatius has to say about the episcopacy and especially about unity, he had the perfect opportunity to insist on a worldwide pontificate for Rome's bishop. Rome was certainly on his mind, since he was traveling there to be martyred as Peter and Paul had been before him.

Yet in his six letters addressed to churches, it is only in his letter to Rome that he does not even mention their bishop (who was probably either St. Evaristus or St. Alexander I). In the other five letters to churches, the bishop is mentioned, and in three of them, the bishop is mentioned by name. When writing to the Roman Christians, he does mention Peter, but equally with Paul as both are apostles who could give them "orders," while Ignatius himself would never presume to do that (*Romans* 4:3). In Ignatius's writings, there is never any special role given to the Roman bishop or the Roman church, nor even to the Apostle Peter. When he writes to Rome, he does not ask the Roman bishop to send a bishop to Antioch to replace him. Rather, he makes that request of Polycarp and his church in Smyrna:

> It is fitting, Polycarp most blessed by God, to summon a council most fit for God which will appoint someone whom you [plural] regard as especially dear to you and zealous, someone who can be called God's courier, and will judge him worthy to go to Syria and glorify your zealous love to the glory of God. (*To Polycarp* 7:2)

He does mention this new vacancy in the Antiochian episcopacy to the Romans, but he says that it now "has God for its shepherd instead of me. Only Jesus Christ will be its bishop—and your love" (*Romans* 9:1).

This absence of support in Ignatius for the modern papacy does not itself constitute a full argument against papal supremacy—it was not an issue in Ignatius's time, so he is not arguing against it. But it is at least a worthwhile data point in considering whether that dogma of the Roman Catholic Church finds support in the early Church. Ignatius does not view Church unity and the bishop in terms of a single administrative head for the whole Church. But what does it mean for Ignatius that the Church is one, especially in terms of the episcopacy? In the next chapter, we will address Church unity in general, including the episcopacy, but let's now focus specifically on the episcopacy itself as the center of unity.

In three separate places, Ignatius writes that he met whole congregations in the persons of their bishops. To the Ephesians, he says, "I received your whole congregation in God's name in the person of Onesimus, a man of inexpressible love and (humanly speaking) your bishop" (*Ephesians* 1:3a). In the bishop Onesimus, Ignatius received the Church of Ephesus—not just one man, but the "whole congregation."

To the Magnesians, he writes, "I was judged worthy of seeing you through Damas your Godworthy bishop and the worthy presbyters Bassus and Apollonius and my fellow slave the deacon Zotion" (*Magnesians* 2:1a). Here Ignatius again identifies a whole church with its bishop Damas. Yet Damas's unity with the Magnesian Christians is not exclusive, because these two presbyters and a deacon also bear the congregation with them. Ignatius singles out the deacon, saying that he enjoys him "because he is subject to the bishop as to God's grace and to the presbytery as to the law of Jesus Christ" (*Magnesians* 2:1b). The order of the Church and the ministries of the clergy all depend on each other, but most especially on the bishop.

In his letter to the Trallians, Ignatius says, "Polybius your bishop . . . so warmly congratulated me—a prisoner in Christ Jesus—that I saw your whole congregation in him. I received your godly love through him and gave God glory because I found you to be (as I knew you were) imitators of God" (*Trallians* 1:1b–2). It was the warmth and love of Polybius that communicated to Ignatius the love of the Church of Tralles. Ignatius believes so much in the oneness of the bishop with his people that he declares them, through Polybius, to be "imitators of God."

Ignatius was clearly impressed with Polybius, as he later says in the same letter, "I have received an embodiment of your love, and have it with me, in your bishop, whose demeanor is a great lesson and whose gentleness is his power. I think even the godless revere him" (*Trallians* 3:2b).

For Ignatius, the bishop therefore not only represents his church as an agent, but he re-presents his church—his whole congregation is in him. He is not over them. In a mystical sense, he *is* them. Ignatius says that the Ephesian presbytery "is attuned to the bishop like strings to a lyre" (*Ephesians* 4:1), an image of a single musical instrument with different parts yet a common, harmonious purpose. In that same epistle, he also says that he considers the Ephesian Christians blessed in that they are "mingled" with their bishop "as Jesus Christ is with the Father" (*Ephesians* 5:1b).

The congregation has this unity with the bishop precisely because of the unity of God and because all are following God and keeping His commandments. Ignatius uses the image of the well-tuned instrument again in his letter to the Philadelphians, but this time, he is talking about the bishop: "For he is attuned to the commandments as a harp is to its strings. Therefore my soul blesses his godly mind, recognizing it as virtuous and perfect, and his immovability and freedom from wrath, with all the gentleness characteristic of the living God" (*Philadelphians* 1:2).

It is the bishop's unity with God that makes possible his unity with the congregation. He provides the "example and lesson in imperishability" (*Magnesians* 6:2); because the bishop is working on his own salvation (becoming imperishable), he shows his flock how to do the same. And it is because "the Lord did nothing apart from the Father"; "since he was united with him, so you must do nothing apart from the bishop and the presbyters" (*Magnesians* 7:1a). The unity of the Father and the Son, of the bishop with God, and of the bishop with the clergy and the people are all deeply connected.

This same unity is expressed with another image in the eleventh chapter of Ignatius's letter to the Trallians:

> Flee from the wicked offshoots which bear deadly fruit; if a man tastes them he soon dies. These are not the planting of the Father. For if they were, they would appear as branches of the cross and their fruit would be imperishable. By the cross through his passion he calls upon you who are his members. The head cannot be begotten apart from the members, since God promises union—himself. (*Trallians* 11)

He is speaking here about discerning heretics, since they are cut off from the head of the Church, who is Christ. Yet Christ's begottenness also means that His members also are begotten of God, since He is the head and we are the body. Likewise, the bishop who heads the church is inseparable from the members of that church. For Ignatius, there is no Church at all without the bishop and the other clergy: "For apart from these [that is, the bishop, presbyters, and deacons] no group can be called a church" (*Trallians* 3:1b).

The bishop is integral to the church and, together with his clergy and laity, constitutes the church. There is no possibility for congregationalism as seen in many modern Christian denominations, where pastors are hired and fired by their congregations. There is also no need here for the bishop's submission to a super-hierarch. The bishop with his clergy and people are what make up the local church. All of this is perhaps best expressed in one of Ignatius's exhortations to Polycarp: "Think upon unity, than which nothing is better. Lift up all men, as the Lord lifts you; put up with all in love, as you actually do" (*To Polycarp* 1:2b).

THE LOCUS OF OBEDIENCE: "BE EAGER NOT TO OPPOSE THE BISHOP"

In the Christian faith, obedience is a major element of the spiritual life, and for Ignatius, we express our obedience to God primarily by obedience to the bishop. He exhorts the believers in nearly every church he writes to that they should be obedient to their bishop. The modern democratic mind balks at this idea because our culture has so indoctrinated us with the idea that we should obey no one but our own desires, that anything else constitutes oppression. Nevertheless, we must look closely at Ignatius's understanding of obedience to see its true nature.

First, the bishop in Ignatius's time has no secular power. Ignatius himself is on his way to martyrdom, and his friend Polycarp would also be martyred. In the early second century, anyone who took up the apostolic mantle of the bishop was risking his life. He was not pursuing a life of prestige. Further, Ignatius's exhortation to obedience is an indication that no one is forcing believers into it. This obedience is not the sort owed to a despotic tyrant, based in fear. Rather, this obedience is offered freely to the bishop as to God. It is something one takes upon oneself voluntarily for the sake of one's salvation. That is why Ignatius uses exhortations rather than threats. Keeping this in mind, let's look at what Ignatius has to say about obedience to the bishop.

Near the beginning of his epistle to the Ephesians, Ignatius talks about their bishop Onesimus: "I beseech you by Jesus Christ to love him and, all of you, to be like him. For blessed is he who gave you the gift, worthy as you are, of obtaining such a bishop" (*Ephesians* 1:3b). Onesimus is a gift from God to the Ephesians, and therefore Ignatius calls on them to love him and to imitate him. That really is the character of Christian obedience to the episcopacy—love and imitation in Christ, out of gratitude to God for the gifts He gives.

He also encourages the Ephesians to be united in their obedience: "It is fitting, then, in every way to glorify Jesus Christ, who glorified you, so that you may be made perfect in a single obedience to the bishop and the presbytery and be sanctified in every way" (*Ephesians* 2:2b). Here, their obedience is not only out of gratitude to God but actually helps to accomplish their salvation—their union in obedience enables them to "be sanctified in every way." Likewise, "The Lord forgives all who repent, if they repent and turn toward the unity of God and the council of the bishop" (*Philadelphians* 8:1b).

Ignatius is clear that obedience to the bishop brings salvation in Christ:

> For when you subject yourselves to the bishop as to Jesus Christ, you appear to me to be living not in human fashion but like Jesus Christ, who died for us so that by believing

> in his death you might escape dying. Therefore it is necessary that, as is actually the case, you do nothing apart from the bishop, but be subject also to the presbytery as to the apostles of Jesus Christ, our hope; for if we live in him we shall be found in him. (*Trallians* 2:1–2)

The peace of mind which comes in this obedience to the bishop and his presbytery is indeed what makes it possible for us to be healed by the Eucharist. He says to the Ephesians, "obey the bishop and the presbytery with undisturbed mind, breaking one loaf, which is the medicine of immortality, the antidote which results not in dying but in living forever in Jesus Christ" (*Ephesians* 20:2b). In another place, he says that God will hear our prayers if we listen to the bishop, writing, "Pay attention to the bishop so that God will pay attention to you" (*To Polycarp* 6:1a).

Obedience to the bishop is also connected to obedience to God Himself: "Let us, therefore, be eager not to oppose the bishop, so that we may be subject to God" (*Ephesians* 5:3b). He tells them not just to go along with what the bishop says, but to be "eager" not to oppose him! Likewise, he says to the Philadelphians, "For as many as belong to God and Jesus Christ, these are with the bishop" (*Philadelphians* 3:2a). Already in his time, there are people who make a show of honoring the bishop and yet do not actually obey him. But he could probably have said this in our time, too: "It is fitting, then, not just to be called Christians but to be such—just as some use the title 'bishop' but do everything apart from him. Such men do not seem to me to act in good conscience, since they do not meet validly in accordance with the commandment" (*Magnesians* 4). We are not to be merely polite to the bishop or to show him grudging respect but to do everything with him.

This attitude toward the bishop makes particular sense in the context of his being the local pastor.

Ignatius says this all the more clearly and forcefully to the Smyrnaeans: "It is good to know God and the bishop. He who honors the bishop has been honored by God; he who does anything without the bishop's knowledge worships the devil" (*Smyrnaeans* 9:1b). This is pretty extreme language! But if we consider that worshiping God with the bishop is "validly according to the commandment," and if we also consider that mankind will always be worshiping something, then it makes sense for Ignatius to say that those who worship apart from the bishop are worshiping the devil.

In our own day Orthodox Christians might find it hard to use this passage especially when addressing non-Orthodox Christians. Should we say to them that, because they are acting apart from the Orthodox episcopacy, they are worshiping the devil? Almost certainly not! But I don't think we should refrain from saying that to them merely because we want to be nice. Rather, we are dealing with a different context than Ignatius was. In his time, the episcopacy was true everywhere. I am not aware of any heretical bishops in his time, so it was literally the case that only with the bishop could a Christian not be a heretic. One could be with the bishop, with the heretics, or with the Jews or pagans. Those were the choices.

At the same time, we can apply Ignatius's words to our time. Because we are worshiping beings, if we want to worship the one true God, then we have to do it "according to the commandment." We cannot make up worship for ourselves. If we do, then we are acting out of pride, and he who acts out of pride indeed is a worshiper of the devil. In that sense, we are all devil-worshipers at one point or another. It is only with humility that we can worship God truly, and humility always involves obedience.

Ignatius says that the obedience that we give to the bishop is divinely ordained. It is not his idea, nor does it come from the ideas of men. To the Philadelphians, he says, "I spoke with a loud voice, God's own voice: 'Pay attention to the bishop and the presbytery and the deacons,'" and also, "The Spirit made proclamation, saying this: 'Do nothing apart from the bishop; keep your flesh as the temple of God; love unity; flee from divisions; be imitators of Jesus Christ as he is of his Father'" (*Philadelphians* 7:1b, 2b).

IN THE PLACE OF GOD: "JUST AS WHEREVER JESUS CHRIST IS"

If Ignatius has so much to say to Christians about obedience to the bishop, he also has much to say about who the bishop must be. Over and over, his imagery for the bishop is of one who is called to stand in the place of God. So if we have much to live up to in terms of obedience, the bishop has even more.

Earlier, we quoted Ignatius's famous saying, "Wherever the bishop appears, the whole congregation is to be present, just as wherever Jesus Christ is, there is the whole Church" (*Smyrnaeans* 8:2). In this comparison, we see the model for Ignatius's picture of the episcopacy. Where the bishop is, the congregation is to be gathered for worship, just as wherever Jesus Christ is, there is the whole Church (literally "the catholic Church").

If it is Christ who makes the whole Church present, then it is the bishop who makes the local church present. The bishop serves as Christ. He is not His vicar, a representative sent by an absent Lord, but serves as an analog who communicates who God is.

This kind of language is everywhere in Ignatius's letters, such as when he writes to the Ephesians, "For everyone whom the master of a house sends for his stewardship, we must receive as the one who sent him. It is obvious, then, that one must look upon the bishop as the Lord himself" (*Ephesians* 6:1b). Here, Ignatius says simply that the bishop is to be looked upon "as the Lord himself" but does not specify whether he means only Christ, the Father, etc. This variation is to be found throughout the epistles.

In the quote above from *Smyrnaens*, the bishop is as Christ, but elsewhere Ignatius says he is worthy of "full respect in accordance with the power of God the Father" (*Magnesians* 3:1b). Likewise, the believers may be compared to Christ and all of the clergy to the Father: "As, then, the Lord did nothing apart from the Father . . . since he was united with him, so you must do nothing apart from the bishop and the presbyters" (*Magnesians* 7:1a).

He also compares *both* the bishop and fellow believers to the Father, writing, "Be subject to the bishop and to one another, as Jesus Christ [in the flesh] was subject to the Father and the apostles were subject to Christ [and the Father], so that there may be unity both fleshly and spiritual" (*Magnesians* 13:2).

Here, the bishop is the Father, but so are one's fellow believers; likewise, Christians are Christ, but they are also the apostles.

In another place, Ignatius likens the bishop not to one of the Persons of the Trinity but rather to God's grace, referring to "the deacon Zotion, whom may I enjoy because he is subject to the bishop as to God's grace and to the presbytery as to the law of Jesus Christ" (*Magnesians* 2:1b). He also compares the deacons to Christ, the bishop to the Father, and the presbyters both to "the council of God" and "the band of the apostles" (*Trallians* 3:1). So we can see that Ignatius has no intentions of setting up a one-to-one allegorical correspondence between any earthly member of the Church and the heavenly realities that the Church makes present.

Therefore, the bishop connects us not to himself but to God. Ignatius, when encouraging the Magnesian Christians to obey their bishop, says, "yield to him—not to him but to the Father of Jesus Christ, the bishop of all. For the honor of him who loved us, it is fitting for us to obey without any hypocrisy; for a man does not deceive only this visible bishop but also cheats the invisible one" (*Magnesians* 3:1b–2a). The obedience we give the bishop is obedience given not to the person of the bishop but to God. This is because the bishop presides "in the place of God" (*Magnesians* 6:1).

Ignatius has a lot to say about how the bishop must behave in order to preside in the place of God. He says much of it in his letter to his friend Polycarp, which is only fitting, since it is the only one of his epistles addressed not to a church, but to one man, who is a bishop. In his salutation, as we quoted earlier, he describes Polycarp as "one who has God the Father and the Lord Jesus Christ as his bishop." And we can probably safely say that all of his exhortations about how believers are to behave toward their bishop therefore apply to how the bishop is to be toward his own "bishop," that is, toward God.

Ignatius tells Polycarp that he must "exhort all men so that they may be saved," that he has to live rightly by his office "with all care both fleshly and spiritual" (*To Polycarp* 1:2). He should also ask God for more understanding than he has and "watch with a sleepless spirit" (1:3). Likewise, he must pastor all appropriately, speaking "to each individual after the example of God" (1:3), not only loving "good disciples," but also bringing "the more troublesome into subjection by gentleness" (2:1). Ignatius also specifically mentions gentleness as an episcopal virtue in his letters to the Trallians (3:2), where he says their bishop's gentleness "is his power," and the Philadelphians, whose bishop, because of his gentleness, "when silent can do more than those who speak in vain" (1:1). As with so much concerning the bishop, this trait is also "characteristic of the living God" (*Philadelphians* 1:2).

It is this gentleness, he tells Polycarp, that enables the bishop to be able to "deal gently with what appears before your face," and he is both fleshly and spiritual for that reason (*To Polycarp* 2:2). The gentleness of the spirit is made manifest in the flesh. But he has to "attain to God, just as pilots seek winds and the storm-tossed sailor a harbor" (2:3). The bishop is called to be one who steers the church appropriately, defending it against "strange doctrine" (3:1) and "evil arts" (5:1). He has to "understand the times" by waiting "for him who is above a moment of time" (3:2). In that, the bishop brings Him who is eternal into the temporal, earthly reality of Christian life.

Polycarp must also defend the widows, being their "guardian" (4:1), and he should also be kind to slaves, while not letting them take advantage of the church's money to buy their earthly freedom (4:3). He is to counsel husbands and wives to live appropriately in their marriages (5:1) while also keeping humble those who choose celibacy (5:2). In all these things, as well, the bishop stands in the place of God, ministering to the various members of his flock in ways appropriate to them.

"DO NOTHING WITHOUT GOD"

All of this makes for a vigorous image of the episcopacy, that it is ordained by God Himself, that believers should give the bishop obedience as they would give it to God, and so forth. But lest we be tempted to think that this is some sort of oppressive, absolute patriarchy, Ignatius reminds Polycarp, "Nothing is to be done without your approval, and you must do nothing without God" (*To Polycarp* 4:1b).

The bishop's position is not about power. It is about service. He and all the clergy are called to be "with God" in everything. They have no power or authority of themselves—their ministry exists only within and for the Church. It does not belong to them personally. If any of the clergy depart from God, then their ministry is powerless and their authority rendered void.

The bishop stands in the place of God, so let us consider what we see God doing in scripture, in icons, and elsewhere: He is serving the Eucharist, preaching the Gospel, healing the sick, lifting up the fallen, and giving hope to the hopeless. That is the episcopacy. That is the priesthood. That is the diaconate.

It is not about controlling people's lives but about coming together to worship the one true God and being healed by Him. That is where the bishop and his clergy find their fulfillment. That is where they are who they truly are. Any bishop, priest, or deacon who trades in his altar for a desk has lost sight of the priesthood. And all believers share in that priesthood. Though not all of us stand next to the altar, we are all called to offer up the one sacrifice to the One who was sacrificed for us, "for if we live in him we shall be found in him" (*Trallians* 2:2).

To close this chapter and to help us understand it in terms of our own experience in the Church, I wanted to comment on something I've mentioned before. In Ignatius's period, the bishop was the local pastor. There are hints at a developing geographic episcopacy, where a bishop is responsible for multiple congregations, each led on his behalf by a presbyter (priest), but that order had not developed very much yet. In our own time, Orthodox churches use this more developed order, so the bishop is usually not the one celebrating the Eucharist every Sunday and managing the parish in its day-to-day life.

But much of what Ignatius says about the bishop, especially unity with the bishop and obedience to him, can be applied appropriately to the bishop's local representative, the presbyter. We should be attuned to our local parish priest just as Ignatius urges us to be attuned to the bishop. He does not have the same kind of apostolic authority as the bishop, but he is nevertheless the bishop's presence for us in our everyday spiritual life.

This may grate against modern sensibilities, which tend to

be distrustful of authority. We don't like the idea of being obedient to anyone but ourselves. And while it may be easier to imagine ourselves obedient to a faraway bishop whom we see at our parish only occasionally, it is more difficult to offer obedience to the man who stands at our parish altars regularly, who knows us well and whose own flaws we can see. But it is only in that relationship of love and chosen obedience that we can experience the benefits of the unity with the bishop that Ignatius describes.

Experience has taught me that the average parish priest pours himself out for his flock, sacrificing not only himself but also quite often the good of his family. I have been grateful for the priests who have given freely to me out of their love. Is this not a father whom we should want to love in return and to whom we can offer even our obedience?

∽ CHAPTER FOUR ∾

The Unity of the Church

The unity of the Church is a key theme for Ignatius, and he speaks of it in nearly all of his letters. For Ignatius, salvation is impossible without unity, and so unity is essential to ecclesiology. It is at the heart of what the Church is and therefore at the heart of what it means to be Christian.

Unity is an all-encompassing, holistic characteristic of ecclesial life. It is not necessary only in, for instance, Church government, liturgy, or doctrine. The Church's unity is to be found in all aspects of Christian life—the dogmatic core of the faith and defense against heresy, the ministry of the clergy, worship, the common life of the believers (especially in their prayer), and in the faith and heart of all those who belong to Christ. For Ignatius, there is no Church, no Christianity without unity.

"BY YOUR UNITY . . . JESUS CHRIST IS SUNG"

In one passage in his epistle to the Ephesians, Ignatius describes Church life as a kind of song, whose pitch comes from God, whose content is Christ, and whose recipient is the Father:

> Therefore it is fitting for you to run your race together with the bishop's purpose—as you do. For your presbytery—worthy of fame, worthy of God—is attuned to the bishop like strings to a lyre. Therefore by your unity and harmonious love Jesus Christ is sung. Each of you must be part of this chorus so that, being harmonious in unity, receiving God's pitch in unison, you may sing with one voice through Jesus Christ to the Father, so that he may both hear you and recognize you, through what you do well, as members of his Son. Therefore it is profitable for you to be in blameless unison, so that you may always participate in God. (*Ephesians* 4:1–2)

This image of the ecclesial song is a beautiful introduction to Ignatius's thoughts on unity, for in one clear picture he paints for us what it means to be a Christian. We as the Church are to be one in all things, at one with the clergy, especially the bishop, loving Christ, receiving from God how we are to live, becoming members of Christ, and in doing so, participating in God.

This theology of unity and of salvation contrasts significantly both with the disunity found in the modern Protestant world—in which ecclesiology usually takes a muted position—and with the Roman Catholic world, in which unity consists mainly in subjection to a single worldwide papacy.

For Ignatius unity is neither irrelevant, as it is for most Protestants, nor to be found in the genius of centralized organization, as it is for Roman Catholics. Rather, its origins are with the Holy Spirit Himself. In his letter to the Philadelphians, Ignatius recalls an incident when he was with them:

When I was with you I cried out, I spoke with a loud voice, God's own voice: "Pay attention to the bishop and the presbytery and the deacons." Some suspected me of saying this because I had advance information about the division of some persons; but he for whom I am in bonds is my witness that I did not know it from any human being. The Spirit made proclamation, saying this: "Do nothing apart from the bishop; keep your flesh as the temple of God; love unity; flee from divisions; be imitators of Jesus Christ as he is of his Father." (*Philadelphians* 7:1b–2)

Elsewhere, he goes so far as to say that division is a sign of the absence of God: "God does not dwell where there is division and wrath" (*Philadelphians* 8:1). True repentance leads instead to unity, both in the heart with God and in the body with the bishop: "The Lord forgives all who repent, if they repent and turn toward the unity of God and the council of the bishop" (ibid.). He also says, "And as many as repent and come to the unity of the church, these also belong to God so that they may be living in accordance with Jesus Christ" (*Philadelphians* 3:2). If there is no unity, then there is no repentance, and therefore there can be no Christianity.

UNITY OF DOCTRINE: "FLEE FROM DIVISION AND WRONG TEACHING"

One of the marks of Christianity for Ignatius is unity in doctrine, specifically doctrine about Jesus Christ. If someone does not believe in the true teachings of the apostles, especially the true humanity of Christ, then he is not really a Christian. But the oneness of Christ with His Father and the oneness of the believer with Christ will yield a oneness of doctrine and a oneness of Christian life between believers.

Someone who is divisive, promoting his own teachings against what comes in the Church, is not truly a follower of Christ. Ignatius says, "I exhort you to do nothing with a partisan spirit—instead, in accordance with what you have learned of Christ" (*Philadelphians* 8:2a). Someone who truly learns who Christ is will not have "a partisan spirit" but will be in unity with the Church. Likewise, someone who behaves in a partisan manner did not learn that from Christ.

Those who try to subvert true doctrine and to divide the Church should be avoided: "As children of the light of truth, flee from division and wrong teaching; where the shepherd is, follow there as sheep. For there are many specious wolves who by evil pleasure take captive those who are running for God; but they will have no place in your unity" (*Philadelphians* 2:1–2).

The only defense against such people is humility and union with Christ and the bishop, following the way of life given by the apostles. He writes, "Be on guard against such men. This will be the case for you if you are not puffed up but are inseparable from the God Jesus Christ and the bishop and the ordinances of the apostles" (*Trallians* 7:1). The proper defense against heresy is, in short, to live the life of a real Christian. But why does correct doctrine matter?

Salvation itself is at stake here, Ignatius writes to the Philadelphians, saying, "'Do not be deceived, my brothers': if anyone follows a maker of schism he 'will not inherit the kingdom of God'; if anyone walks in strange doctrine he has no share in the passion" (*Philadelphians* 3:3). If we want to share in Christ's Passion and what it accomplishes for us, then we cannot "walk in strange doctrine."

For Ignatius, heresy is like poison: "I exhort you therefore—not I but the love of Jesus Christ—use only Christian food and abstain from every strange plant, which is heresy. For they mingle Jesus Christ with themselves, feigning faith, providing something like a deadly drug with honeyed wine, which the ignorant man gladly takes with pleasure; and therein is death" (*Trallians* 6:1–2). True doctrine matters because heresy is dangerous to spiritual health. It is death. We have to be on guard to remain in the Church's doctrinal unity, because heresy is tempting and even pleasurable, yet nevertheless deadly.

When writing to the Philadelphians, he likens heretics to bad plants in God's garden: "Abstain from evil weeds which Jesus Christ does not cultivate because they are not the planting of the Father" (*Philadelphians* 3:1a). At the same time, he assures the Philadelphians that he did not find division in their midst. What he found was "filtering-out" (3:1b)—that is, they were weeding their garden.

Elsewhere, he says,

> It is fitting to keep away from such men and not to speak about them either privately or publicly, but to pay attention to the prophets and especially to the gospel, in which the passion has been explained to us and the resurrection has been accomplished. Flee from divisions as the beginning of evils. (*Smyrnaeans* 7:2)

He says that these heretics even refrained from receiving the Eucharist, because they did not believe it was truly Christ's Body and Blood. What greater division can there be than to be voluntarily excommunicated?

Ignatius urges believers to "be deaf, then, when anyone speaks to you apart from Jesus Christ . . . without whom we have no true life" (*Trallians* 9:1–2). The question of doctrinal unity, specifically unity in true doctrine, is for Ignatius a matter of spiritual life and death. Heresy is not merely someone's honest opinion but is "deadly." At the same time, the true faith in Jesus Christ gives true life. Spiritual health requires correct doctrine.

In his epistle to the Magnesians, Ignatius writes, "Do not try to make anything appear praiseworthy by yourselves, but let there be in common one prayer, one petition, one mind, one hope in love, in blameless joy—which is Jesus Christ, than whom nothing is better" (*Magnesians* 7:1b). There is no private Christianity because of who Jesus is, the "blameless joy" in whom all these things are commonly held as one. He continues, "All of you must run together as to one temple of God, as to one sanctuary, to one Jesus Christ, who proceeded from the one Father and is with the one and departed to the one" (*Magnesians* 7:2). The oneness that Jesus has with His Father is the source of the unity that Christians have with each other.

And it is not only the Son's unity with the Father that is the source of Christian unity. Christ's identity as a real human man is key to the Christian's ability to have life. We should only listen to the true doctrine about Jesus, who was of the family of David, who was of Mary, who was truly born, ate and drank, was truly persecuted under Pontius Pilate, was truly crucified and died, while heavenly, earthly, and subterranean beings looked on. He was also truly raised from the dead, when his Father raised him up, as in similar fashion his Father will raise up in Christ Jesus us who believe him—without whom we have no true life. (*Trallians* 9:1b–2)

It is only with faith in the true identity of Christ, rather than in heretical doctrines, that we will enjoy the full fruits of the Resurrection.

UNITY IN THE CLERGY: "SO THAT ALL THINGS ARE HARMONIOUS"

All the clergy together are an integral element of church unity for Ignatius—the bishop, the presbytery, and the diaconate. There can be no unity without following the bishop and the other clergy.

In one place, he even says that there is no Church without them, as when he says to the Trallians, "All are to respect the deacons as Jesus Christ and the bishop as a copy of the Father and the presbyters as the council of God and the band of the apostles. For apart from these no group can be called a church" (*Trallians* 3:1). He also says that if one truly belongs to God, then he is also going to belong to the bishop: "For as many as belong to God and Jesus Christ, these are with the bishop" (*Philadelphians* 2:1a). There is no Church without the congregation surrounding the bishop, the presbyters, and the deacons.

In his letter to the Ephesians, Ignatius mentions the time he spent with their bishop Onesimus and how blessed the spiritual communion with him was:

> For if in a short time I had such fellowship with your bishop as was not human but spiritual, how much more blessed do I consider you who are mingled with him as the Church is with Jesus Christ and as Jesus Christ is with the Father, so that all things are harmonious in unison! (*Ephesians* 5:1)

For Ignatius, the unity that is centered on the bishop is not a unity whose basis is organization or structure. Rather, the believers are "mingled" with their bishop.

He identifies two kinds of "mingling" that the unity between the bishop and believers should imitate—Christ with the Church and Christ with the Father.

In the first, Christ and the Church, it is a mingling which has Christ as the head of the Church. In the Church, believers are united to Him especially in His eucharistic Body and Blood, and they become His ecclesial Body. Likewise, the bishop gives of himself to the believers under his care, and he is also their head but inseparable from them. He is not above his church but part of it.

In the second kind of "mingling," Ignatius wants the Ephesians to be one with their bishop as the Son of God is one with His Father. In that union of the Father and Son, there is total equality yet nevertheless hierarchy, a perfect communion of Persons who agree in everything and do everything together.

This is the kind of order Ignatius has in mind, a divinely breathed order in which the clergy's unity with the laity is founded on the unity of God the Father, Son, and Holy Spirit. He frequently compares the hierarchy and unity of the Church with the hierarchy and unity of the Godhead, as well as with the community that Jesus formed with His apostles.

Typical are these words to the Magnesians:

> I exhort you: be eager to do everything in God's harmony, with the bishop presiding in the place of God and the presbytery in the place of the council of the apostles and the deacons, most sweet to me, entrusted with the service of Jesus Christ—who before the ages was with the Father and was made manifest at the end. (*Magnesians* 6:1b)

He makes these comparisons in various ways, and they are not strictly arranged as an allegory, where the bishop is always God, the presbytery the apostles, and so forth. In another place, he tells the Magnesians, "Be subject to the bishop and to one another, as Jesus Christ [in the flesh] was subject to the Father and the apostles were subject to Christ [and the Father], so that there may be unity both fleshly and spiritual" (*Magnesians* 13:2). Here, the believers are to be like Christ and the bishop as the Father, but the believers are also to be like the apostles, and the bishop as Christ.

His point is that the Magnesians should be

> eager, therefore, to be firmly set in the decrees of the Lord and his apostles so that "in whatever you do you may prosper"—in flesh and spirit, in faith and love, in the Son and the Father and in the Spirit, at the beginning and at the end, together with your right reverend bishop and that worthily woven spiritual crown, your presbytery, and the godly deacons. (*Magnesians* 13:1)

His language is so beautifully intertwined here, especially with the wonderful image of the presbytery as a "worthily woven spiritual crown," that we come away with an organic, rather than institutional, image of what the Church is. It is at once Trinitarian, hierarchical, bodily, spiritual, doctrinal, apostolic, loving, and faithful.

He writes in another place to the Magnesians, "Let there be nothing in you that can divide you, but be united with the bishop and with those who preside, for an example and lesson of imperishability" (*Magnesians* 6:2b). Again, his purpose is their salvation, which he identifies here as "imperishability," that is, being free of death. He also presumes that "those who preside" are actually capable of giving an "example and lesson of imperishability." They have to be working on their own salvation in order to be an example and in order to be able to teach that lesson.

He connects perfection and imperishability to unity with the clergy in another place, when he writes to the Ephesians, "It is fitting, then, in every way to glorify Jesus Christ, who glorified you, so that you may be made perfect in a single obedience to the bishop and the presbytery and be sanctified in every respect" (*Ephesians* 2:2b). This is one of the ministries of the clergy in the Church.

At the same time, he also identifies a ministry that the Church should do for the bishop, writing to the Trallians, "It is fitting for each of you, especially the presbyters, to refresh the bishop, to the honor of the Father, Jesus Christ, and the apostles" (*Trallians* 12:2b). He says this after mentioning that the churches visiting him had refreshed him in both body and spirit (12:1). Clearly, it would have been easier to "refresh the bishop" in Ignatius's time, when he was the local pastor, but the principle still holds, both for one's local pastor and also for the archpastor, the bishop himself.

UNITY IN WORSHIP: "HE WHO IS WITHIN THE SANCTUARY IS PURE"

Although it is clear from Ignatius's writings that unity with the clergy is critical to unity in the Church, the clergy's purpose is not really administrative. Rather, their ordinations are for serving in worship. He writes concerning deacons, "Those who are deacons of the mysteries of Jesus Christ must please all men in every way. For they are not ministers of food and drink but servants of the church of God" (*Trallians* 2:3a).

There is something of a pun to be found here, if we look underneath the translation. *Diakonos*, the Greek basis for our English word "deacon," means "servant" but more precisely "waiter," that is, one who waits tables. So Ignatius is saying that the deacons are not ordinary table servants, but servants of the Church, servants of the mysteries of Jesus Christ. Why would he say this? It is because in the earliest known liturgical practice, the Eucharist was served to the people by the deacons. What the deacons are giving to the people is not just food and drink but something much more. But all the clergy, even bishops and presbyters, qualify in this sense as deacons, for they who serve the mysteries of Christ are servants of the Church of God.

Worship under the direction of the bishop is critical to the Christian life, and anyone who does not participate in it has removed himself from the Church: "Therefore he who does not come to the assembly is already proud and has separated himself. For it is written, 'God opposes the proud.' Let us, therefore, be eager not to oppose the bishop, so that we may be subject to God" (*Ephesians* 5:3). If we want to be subject to God, we cannot be at odds with the bishop.

This identification of the clergy with the liturgical worship of the Church is also affirmed when Ignatius writes, "He who is within the sanctuary is pure; he who is outside the sanctuary is not pure—that is, whoever does anything apart from the bishop and the presbytery and the deacons is not pure in conscience" (*Trallians* 7:2). Doing things apart from the clergy is standing outside the sanctuary, and thus outside the Church, because it is in the sanctuary that purity comes. There, sins are forgiven and consciences cleansed.

Likewise, he also writes, "Let no one deceive himself: unless a man is within the sanctuary, he lacks the bread of God. If the prayer of one or two has such power, how much more does that of the bishop and the whole church?" (*Ephesians* 5:2). The "bread of God," which is the Eucharist, is only to be found in the sanctuary.

Interestingly, the word which is translated in both of these references as "sanctuary" is the Greek *thysiastirion*, which is most commonly translated as "altar," but literally means "place of sacrifice" or "place of offering" (from *thysia*, "sacrifice" or "offering"). Ignatius is not only talking about a space used by Christians for worship in a general sense but rather a place where sacrifices are offered up, the sacrifice of the Eucharist.

The Eucharist is a powerful, potent force for the Church. Ignatius therefore says, when writing to the Ephesians, that they should "be eager to meet more frequently for thanksgiving [*eucharistian*] and glory to God. For when you frequently come together, the powers of Satan are destroyed and his destructive force is annihilated by the concord of your faith" (*Ephesians* 13:1). The act of coming together frequently for the Eucharist unifies the Church.

The unity at the Eucharist is a major element of its character. The sacrament is not objectified outside the context of the assembly, the synaxis for worship and for communing. The Eucharist is for communing together as the Body of Christ, not for private devotion and worship. It is also why the Divine Liturgy may never be served alone. There must be a coming together of Christians, even if it is only one priest and one altar server.

Writing to the Ephesians, Ignatius says believers should each make the choice to join together. He hopes that the Lord reveals to him

> that individually you are all joining, by grace from the Name, in one faith and in Jesus Christ, who was of the family of David after the flesh, son of man and Son of

> God, so that you may obey the bishop and the presbytery with undisturbed mind, breaking one loaf, which is the medicine of immortality, the antidote which results not in dying but in living forever in Jesus Christ. (*Ephesians* 20:2)

Again, we have many elements of Christian unity bound up in one beautiful statement. Here is the "one faith" in the true God-man Jesus Christ, in obedience to the bishop and presbyters, breaking the one eucharistic loaf, which is the "medicine of immortality." The Eucharist is one because Christ is one, and therefore the Church must be one and its doctrine must be one.

Ignatius writes something quite similar to the Philadelphians:

> Be eager, therefore, to use one Eucharist—for there is one flesh of our Lord Jesus Christ and one cup for union with his blood, one sanctuary, as there is one bishop, together with the presbytery and the deacons my fellow slaves—so that, whatever you do, you do it in relation to God. (*Philadelphians* 4)

It is because of this thoroughgoing unity that the Orthodox Church cannot share Holy Communion with anyone who is not Orthodox. In one of those areas—whether it is having a separate faith, a separate bishop, or a separate altar, or something else—we have a discontinuity with those who are not one with us. It is not because we do not love the non-Orthodox and do not want to share in communion with them, but that communion is only possible if we really are one.

Some may object that love should overlook such disunity. But that kind of "love" disregards everything else Ignatius is saying. If the Eucharist really is the "medicine of immortality," if opposing the bishop means opposing God, if heretical doctrines are deadly, then how can we call overlooking disunity "love"? Ignatius praises the Magnesians at the opening of his letter to them, saying, "When I learned of the orderliness of your love toward God, I gladly decided to speak with you in the faith of Jesus Christ . . . I sing of the churches and I pray that in them there may be a union of the flesh and spirit of Jesus Christ, our life forever" (*Magnesians* 1:1–2a). It is only in the "orderliness" of unity that love can be real, that it can unite us together in the flesh and spirit of Christ.

"WITH UNDIVIDED HEART"

Perhaps the most plaguing characteristic of our times is that we are fragmented people with a fragmented culture. And here is St. Ignatius of Antioch urging us in every way toward unity. It may seem like an elusive goal. Especially in a culture that celebrates diversity without unity, we are surrounded by people who find the idea irrelevant to begin with. But within the soul of each human person is the need for a particular kind of love. Ignatius encourages the Trallian Christians to take on this love and make it their own, writing, "And each of you must love one another with undivided heart" (*Trallians* 13:2b).

What does it mean for us to have "undivided" hearts? We have been hearing what Ignatius would say about that. It is manifest in unity of doctrine, unity with the clergy, and unity in worship. But it is not as though these unities are a kind of checklist which, if we fulfill them all, guarantee us that our hearts are undivided. We could manifest them in a formal, outward way, yet still be broken people.

Christian love should exhibit a common life in prayer: "My bonds exhort you, bonds which I bear for Jesus Christ, praying that I may reach God: continue in your harmony and in prayer with one another" (*Trallians* 12:2). People who "continue in . . . harmony and in prayer with one another" are not going to be normal in this world. The world teaches us to compete with one another, to dominate one another. It certainly does not teach us to pray for or with each other. In thinking about his beloved Antioch and Syria, which were in his episcopal care but are now losing their father to the lions in Rome, he beseeches the Magnesian Christians:

> Since I know you are full of God I have exhorted you briefly. Remember me in your prayers so that I may attain to God, and remember the church in Syria, from which I am not worthy to be called. For I need your united prayer in God and your love so that the church in Syria may be judged worthy of being refreshed with the dew from your church. (*Magnesians* 14)

Ignatius also stresses that our inner convictions be united to God, which enables us to love each other in a way that transcends normal human behavior: "All of you, then, having received a divine agreement in your convictions, admonish one another, and let no one view his neighbor in a merely human way; but constantly love one another in Jesus Christ. Let there be nothing in you that can divide you" (*Magnesians* 6:2). If we live this way, then we can even see our neighbor with the eyes of faith. Real love that comes from God is not possible if we continue to look at one another "in a merely human way."

Ignatius even says that the Church can bring together people of disparate cultures and languages. He identifies Christianity as the place "in which 'every language' believing in God was 'brought together'" (*Magnesians* 10:3b). No doubt he is here thinking of the Day of Pentecost, on which language was no longer a barrier between people, but everyone heard the preaching of the apostles in his own language. The Church is a new nation, the race of Christians.

Christians are a different kind of people, and Ignatius expects to see unity when he writes, "Labor together with one another, strive together, run together, suffer together, rest together, rise up together—as God's stewards and assistants and servants" (*To Polycarp* 6:1a). This kind of unity is something the world rarely sees, yet the martyr-bishop of Antioch expects it when he looks at Christians.

Perhaps a fitting conclusion and summary of all that we have observed in the writings of St. Ignatius on the question of unity in the Church may be found in one of his wonderful, all-encompassing passages that seem to teach everything all at once. In his final farewell in his letter to the whole community of Smyrnaean Christians, he writes this:

> I salute the bishop, worthy of God, and the presbytery, fit for God, and my fellow slaves the deacons and all of you,

individually and together, in the name of Jesus Christ and in his flesh and blood, his passion and resurrection both fleshly and spiritual, in union with God and with you. Grace be to you, mercy, peace, endurance forever. (*Smyrnaeans* 12:2)

~: CHAPTER FIVE :~

The Eucharist

St. Ignatius of Antioch forcefully insists, again and again, on the reality of the fleshly humanity of Jesus Christ. As we saw earlier, one of his major concerns is the ongoing struggle against the docetists, those heretics who believed in the divinity of Jesus but not His humanity. They said that He only *appeared* to be a man, though of course He was God.

It is on this basis that they refrained from the Eucharist, for if God had not come in the flesh, why receive the (supposed) flesh of Christ in church? They were right to connect the Incarnation to the Eucharist, as we shall see more below. But they were wrong to abstain from communing, because they were wrong about who Jesus was. Ignatius refutes them by saying that, if He is not truly man, then how can we possibly be clothed with Him, putting on Christ in baptism, as St. Paul says in Galatians 3:27? Someone who denies the flesh of Jesus, Ignatius says, has "absolutely denied him and is clothed with a corpse" (*Smyrnaeans* 5:2).

The Incarnation is a powerful, ever-present reality for Ignatius, and everything hangs on it. Without the reality of both the divinity and the humanity of Jesus Christ, then there really is no point in being Christian. Those who deny Christ's humanity violate the very foundation of the Church's faith. In our own time, we can say the same thing about those who deny His divinity.

"YOU ARE BOTH FLESHLY AND SPIRITUAL"

For Ignatius, the union between flesh and spirit is so critical that he uses the phrase "flesh and spirit" (or on a few occasions "fleshly and spiritual") no fewer than fourteen times in his seven epistles, at least once in each of them. Spiritual and fleshly reality come together to us as Christ, and that same union is also to be found in Christians and everything they do pertaining to Christ.

With Ignatius's dedication to the divine-human identity of Christ and the intimate union of flesh and spirit, it makes sense that he would also be dedicated to the reality of the Eucharist—that in the Divine Liturgy bread and wine truly become the Body and Blood of Christ. Christians for centuries have always made this natural connection, that the Incarnation has numerous extensions and consequences, but that the most obvious, the most central, the most potent is the truth of the Eucharist.

It is only relatively recently that large numbers of Christians no longer accept this affirmation of faith in the Eucharist. This rejection is not found in the Scriptures or the Church Fathers but rather is based in a sensibility developed in the Protestant churches coming from the Radical Reformation that finding holiness in physical objects is pagan superstition. The preference instead is for "four bare walls and a sermon," and the Christian faith is reduced to something that cannot be touched but only intellectually thought about or emotionally felt.

Traditional Christians, who believe in the intermingling of flesh and spirit that Ignatius so often mentions and of the uncreated God with the created world, might rightly regard this rejection of the physical side of Christian life as a kind of gnosticism or new docetism, in which the spiritual is "real," but anything materially physical must be reducible to mere symbol. Doesn't this rejection of materiality essentially isolate the Incarnation to a singular event that has no impact on the rest of the material world? Did God's interaction with created matter really end when the Son of God became a material man? Or does it not instead make more sense that the Incarnation was the beginning of the redemption of the created world? Would not the union of God and man be best accessible to humanity in his most primal act of connection with the material world—eating?

If it is true that the Son of God became incarnate as a true human man, then giving us His flesh and blood to eat and drink would give us direct access to His saving divinity. This is the logic that Ignatius himself is working from. It is the Apostle John who gives us the clearest and most foundational passage in the New Testament regarding the Eucharist, in the sixth chapter of his Gospel. While Ignatius does not quote directly from John's extant writings, he is still using John's theology. So while Ignatius may not have known this particular passage, we can safely assume that he would have learned about this incident from John. Here are the words of Christ Himself in John:

"Most assuredly, I say to you, he who believes in Me has everlasting life. I am the bread of life. Your fathers ate the manna in the wilderness, and are dead. This is the bread which comes down from heaven, that one may eat of it and not die. I am the living bread which came down from heaven. If anyone eats of this bread, he will live forever; and the bread that I shall give is My flesh, which I shall give for the life of the world."

The Jews therefore quarreled among themselves, saying, "How can this Man give us *His* flesh to eat?"

Then Jesus said to them, "Most assuredly, I say to you, unless you eat the flesh of the Son of Man and drink His blood, you have no life in you. Whoever eats My flesh and drinks My blood has eternal life, and I will raise him up at the last day. For My flesh is food indeed, and My blood is drink indeed. He who eats My flesh and drinks My blood abides in Me, and I in him. As the living Father sent Me, and I live because of the Father, so he who feeds on Me will live because of Me. This is the bread which came down from heaven—not as your fathers ate the manna, and are dead. He who eats this bread will live forever." (John 6:47–58)

Even though Ignatius does not quote this passage (nor anything else from John, as noted in the introduction), we still hear exactly this kind of language echoed in his writings. Christ's flesh and spirit are united, and His Body and Blood, which are food and drink "indeed," therefore communicate to us immortality.

THE EUCHARIST, CHRIST, AND HUMANITY: "BOTH FLESH AND SPIRIT"

As we just said, Ignatius uses the phrase "flesh and spirit" or "fleshly and spiritual" fourteen times in his letters. In every instance, the two Greek words used are *sarx* and *pneuma*. Let's look at these words to see what Ignatius might mean by them.

First, in using *sarx*, Ignatius is drawing directly on the language of Christ Himself as we quoted from John's Gospel. Christ uses *sarx* when speaking of His flesh. It is translated as "flesh" but also sometimes as "body." *Sarx* is in any case a physically solid and substantial term. It is not the kind of word you would use if you wanted to be polite. Rather, it is earthy, almost gory. It has the kind of linguistic impact of our English word "meat."

There can be no question as to what Jesus means here. This is His real flesh, and that is what He is giving to Christians to eat. It's no wonder the Jews argued and asked, "How can this Man give us His flesh to eat?" It sounds crazy. Christ's response was to affirm the meatiness: "For My flesh is food indeed, and My blood is drink indeed." In Greek, He literally says, "My flesh is true food," and, "My blood is true drink." He emphasizes that His flesh is food and that His blood is drink. He's talking about real eating and drinking.

In certain old translations of John 6 into English, the Greek word used here for "eat," *trogo*, is translated as "craunch," the forerunner of our modern English word "crunch." The Greek *trogo* refers to what you do with your teeth when you're eating uncooked vegetables or nuts. It's very clear that He's talking about real eating!

Pneuma has a much less physical character. It is literally "breath," but it is used here as "spirit." It can mean the Holy Spirit, the spirit of a man, or the spirit of Christ Himself. *Pnevmatikos* is the word translated as "spiritual."

The *pneuma* in both the Scripture and Ignatius's letters is the breath that animates, the power that makes man alive, whether it is the lasting power of God in a person—which is the Holy Spirit—or the inner, immaterial aspect of personhood. This may sometimes also be understood as the "soul," which is *psychi* in Greek, though this is not a word Ignatius emphasizes. Ignatius also uses the phrase "flesh and soul and spirit" (*Philadelphians* 11:2), so there can also be a sense in which the soul that is the person's immaterial aspect may be distinct from the spirit, which could be the Holy Spirit. In any case, Ignatius is more concerned here with the unity (*omonoia*) between "flesh and soul and spirit" than with splitting mankind up into parts.

In some of the writings of the Fathers, there is not consistency in drawing a distinction between soul and spirit. Ignatius mainly uses *pneuma*—spirit. The ambiguity here is perhaps useful: does he mean only the immaterial aspect of the person himself, or does he mean the Holy Spirit? Sometimes, it may be both. Whatever the case, this phrase "flesh and spirit" (or "fleshly and spiritual") can tell us much about what he has to say on the Eucharist. So let's look at all fourteen instances of it.

In his letter to the Ephesians, Ignatius speaks about the Lord Himself: "There is one Physician: both flesh and spirit; begotten and unbegotten; in man, God; in death, true life; both from Mary and from God; first passible and then impassible; Jesus Christ our Lord" (*Ephesians* 7:2). In this beautiful summary of his Christology, Ignatius primarily emphasizes the oneness of Christ's divinity and humanity.

Yet, within the poetic structure of this verse (which is a chiasmus, forming a forward progression followed by its reverse; see the chiastic illustration of this verse on page 61), the phrase "both flesh and spirit" forms a chiastic connection to the phrase "first passible and then impassible." The flesh is "passible"—it can be acted upon. But the spirit is "impassible"—meaning that it is beyond the mutability of createdness. The Eucharist likewise is both flesh and spirit, both passible and impassible. It is passible because we can eat and drink it but impassible because it is the very flesh and blood of God. And, if we may say so, it is "first" passible because our first experience of it is the eating and drinking, but "then" impassible because it is an experience of the divine.

Ignatius also speaks of this union to the Magnesians: "I sing of the churches and I pray that in them there may be a union of the flesh and spirit of Jesus Christ, our life forever" (*Magnesians* 1:2). The eucharistic sense of that phrase is unmistakable—he is praying for that union of Christ's flesh and spirit in the churches. In the churches, there is literally "a union of the flesh and spirit of Jesus Christ," who is "our life forever." That is one way of reading this phrase.

Vall says that there are several other ways this phrase "union of the flesh and spirit of Jesus Christ" can be taken, depending on how one reads the Greek grammar (Vall, p. 92). It could mean that there is a union "in the domain of flesh and spirit" and that this union comes from Jesus Christ. Likewise, it could mean a union that comes from the flesh and spirit of Jesus Christ.

The ambiguity need not be confusing, because all these meanings are edifying to the reader. Ignatius can be read here to be speaking in terms of the eucharistic union, as I suggest, the actual act of the change of the bread and wine. Or he could be referring to the union among the Magnesians in their flesh and spirit, a union coming from Christ. Or this union could find itself coming from the flesh and spirit of Jesus Christ. All three versions are eucharistic and compatible with one another.

He also salutes the Smyrnaeans at the end of his letter to them: "I salute . . . all of you, individually and together, in the name of Jesus Christ and in his flesh and blood, his passion and resurrection both fleshly and spiritual, in union with God and with you" (*Smyrnaeans* 12:2). Again, notice both the eucharistic reference to Christ's flesh and blood and also the characterization of the Passion and Resurrection as "both fleshly and spiritual."

Jesus did not die and rise again only in His spirit, but also in His flesh, emphasizing the unity of both in the one Person. It is the Person Jesus Christ, the Son of God, who suffered, died, and resurrected, and therefore when we receive His flesh and blood in the Eucharist, we receive the whole Christ Himself—both God and man. We receive not merely a part of Him or a symbol of Him, but all of Him, and by this means St. Ignatius is able to say that he is "in union with God and with you." The Eucharist is the great link between God and man and between those who are in Christ, and the link is not only possible *because of* Christ—it *is* Christ. He makes the link possible, and He is Himself the link.

At the same time, Ignatius uses the phrase "flesh and spirit" to refer not only to the Lord Jesus but also to those who are uniting to Him. As we saw earlier, he frequently admonishes his readers to be engaged in the spiritual life in both flesh and spirit. To the Ephesians, when urging them to suffer gladly for Christ, he says that in doing so they "may remain in Jesus Christ, in flesh and spirit" (*Ephesians* 10:3). Not only are their spirits to remain in Him, but also their flesh.

And if both flesh and spirit are in Christ, then spiritual life is not just for the spirit but includes the flesh. As he says elsewhere to the Ephesians, "what you do in relation to the flesh is spiritual, for you do everything in Jesus Christ" (*Ephesians* 8:2). You can't do something "in Jesus Christ" that is not spiritual.

In his salutation to the Romans, he says that they are "united in flesh and spirit to every commandment of his [that is, of Christ], filled with God's grace without wavering, and filtered clean of every alien stain" (*Romans*, Salutation). Again, the spiritual life is not a matter only of the spirit but of the flesh. Being united to Christ's commandments is a matter for both our flesh and our spirit. When we obey those commandments in both flesh and spirit, we are "filled with God's grace without wavering, and filtered clean of every alien stain."

A true spiritual life, which includes both the flesh and the spirit, has real effects. It is because of these real effects that Ignatius can tell Polycarp that his ability to pastor is based on his being "both fleshly and spiritual." Polycarp therefore can both "deal gently with what appears before [his] face" and also "ask that invisible things may be made manifest" to him. Because he is both fleshly and spiritual, Polycarp can function in both the visible and invisible realms, so that he will "lack nothing and abound in every gift of grace" (*To Polycarp* 2:2).

Likewise, when writing to the Magnesians, he sets union with God in both flesh and spirit in the larger context of other unities: "in flesh and spirit, in faith and love, in the Son and the Father and in the Spirit, at the beginning and at the end, together with your right reverend bishop and that worthily woven spiritual crown, your presbytery, and the godly deacons" (*Magnesians* 13:1).

To Polycarp, he urges that he teach women in the church to "love the Lord and be content with their husbands, both in flesh and in spirit" (*To Polycarp* 5:1). Here the participation of believers' flesh and spirit is bound up in all the realities of church and family life, thus revealing it as profoundly eucharistic, as uniting all together to God in the Lord Jesus.

That unity of common life is also evident when Ignatius says to the Trallians that those visiting him in Smyrna "in every respect refreshed me in flesh and spirit" (*Trallians* 12:1). Their love for him connected to him in both a fleshly and spiritual way. This says something about our ministry as the Church, not just to a visiting bishop who is about to be martyred, but to anyone who comes to us. Are we refreshing them "in both flesh and spirit"? Some people want the Church to do only one or the other. But we need to do both.

He also prays in his letter to the Smyrnaeans that a certain Tavia will be "established in faith and love both fleshly and spiritual" (*Smyrnaeans* 13:1). We can perhaps conceive of *love* that is "both fleshly and spiritual," but what about a *faith* that is also "both fleshly and spiritual"? Ignatius does not leave faith only to the spirit, but it is also for the flesh. Do we have faithful flesh?

Is our faith "fleshly" as well as "spiritual"? Faith has to be lived in every part of who we are. It is not enough only to believe or to pray privately. We also must have faithful action in the flesh—both practical love for others and also the fleshly actions of corporate prayer and of receiving the Eucharist and all the holy mysteries.

Peace is also found in both the flesh and spirit. In his salutation to the Trallians, Ignatius says that they are "at peace in flesh and spirit through the passion of Jesus Christ our hope through his resurrection" (*Trallians*, Salutation). Here, their "peace in flesh and spirit" is possible because of Christ's suffering and Resurrection, which believers receive most powerfully in the holy Eucharist.

He also depicts the believers' identification with Christ's suffering on the Cross quite directly in writing to the Smyrnaeans: "For I know that you are established in immovable faith, as if you were nailed in flesh and spirit to the cross of the Lord Jesus Christ and confirmed in love by the blood of Christ" (*Smyrnaeans* 1:1). Their faith is immovable, as if their flesh and spirits are nailed to the cross, and they are confirmed in this love by His blood, which they receive in the holy Eucharist. As he says of the apostles, "They immediately touched him and believed, being mingled with his flesh and spirit" (*Smyrnaeans* 3:2).

How do we summarize all this "flesh and spirit" language? It's tough to summarize, because Ignatius uses it in so many ways. He says a lot of things here—the "flesh and spirit" are Christ's as a human man; they are Christ's in His Body and Blood in the Eucharist; and they are ours as human persons uniting with Him and with each other. And what is "fleshly" is also "spiritual." Our faith and love and obedience to Christ must all be "fleshly and spiritual."

I'm not sure that Ignatius's "flesh and spirit" language is really reducible to a single idea or teaching. Nevertheless, an image does emerge from all this that in Christ we have union with God and with each other in a way that is both "fleshly and spiritual," and that this union has much to do with the Holy Eucharist.

THE CHRISTIAN AS THE EUCHARIST: "I AM THE WHEAT OF GOD"

In Ignatius's eucharistic vision of the Church, he not only emphasizes that believers' participation in church life is to be according to both the flesh and the spirit, but he takes this truth further and images the Christian as the Eucharist itself. The Christian is identified with both the Person of Christ and also with the Eucharist. Ignatius applies this image even to himself, particularly in light of his impending martyrdom. In our own day, some Orthodox theologians have referred to the Eucharist as the food that consumes us, rather than being a food that we consume, perhaps echoing St. Augustine who heard God saying to him, "I am the food of grown men. Grow and you shall feed upon Me. And you will not, as with the food of the body, change Me into yourself, but you will be changed into Me" (*Conf.* VII.x.16). That is, while our bodies change most food into us in a biological way, the Eucharist changes us into Christ in a mystical way.

While this kind of language might be surprising, it is no less surprising than the language that Paul uses in Galatians 3:27, saying that we have "put on Christ" in baptism, or in Ephesians, that we are to grow to "the measure of the stature of the fullness of Christ" (Eph. 4:13). If that is not enough, Paul also explicitly makes the identification of the Christian with the Eucharist, united in one Church: "The cup of blessing which we bless, is it not the communion of the blood of Christ? The bread which we break, is it not the communion of the body of Christ? For we, *though* many, are one bread *and* one body; for we all partake of that one bread" (1 Cor. 10:16–17). Because we all partake of that one eucharistic bread, we have become "one bread and one body."

When writing to Polycarp, Ignatius gives a particular example of an identification of one kind of Christian life with the flesh of Christ, the life of celibacy: "If anyone is able to remain in purity, in honor of the Lord's flesh, he must do so without boasting" (*To Polycarp* 5:2a).

Monasticism as such did not yet exist at this point in Church history, but there were already people living in celibacy for the sake of Christ. Jesus even mentions this way of life in Matthew 19:12, saying that those who are able to accept this way of life should do so. Thus, Ignatius refers here to Christ's flesh specifically in terms of the Lord's celibacy, and he says that those who imitate Christ in this way are honoring Him.

But they can do so only in humility. He writes, "If anyone boasts he is lost, and if it is made known to anyone but the bishop, he has been corrupted" (*To Polycarp* 5:2b). Thus, in order to be identified with Christ and to imitate Him in the flesh, one must also imitate Him in the spirit, remaining humble. For Ignatius the identification with Christ *par excellence* is in martyrdom. In speaking of his martyrdom as he urges the Roman Christians not to hinder it, Ignatius famously uses eucharistic language for himself in one of his most-quoted passages: "I am the wheat of God and I am ground by the teeth of wild beasts so that I may be found the pure bread of Christ" (*Romans* 4:1). If in the Eucharist bread becomes flesh, then here, Ignatius says that his flesh is becoming bread. But he begins as wheat that must be ground. It is in his martyrdom, in his suffering that is joined to the suffering of Christ, that he can become that flour that becomes "the pure bread of Christ."

Gregory Vall puts it this way:

> Ignatius's ecclesial-sacramental existence in this life is to be consummated by martyrdom in such a way that he himself, in some sense, becomes eucharist. He even takes this one step further and suggests that he would in that case become "a sacrifice to God." While there is a bit of playfulness in Ignatius's tone at this point in *Romans*, it would be a mistake to toss these expressions aside as mere hyperbole and metaphor. The overall tenor of the letter is, after all, one of great urgency and earnestness. Ignatius's images direct our attention to a profound mystery that deserves careful reflection. (p. 145)

Vall goes on to point out that it is a paradox that the integrity of the human person as both body and soul must be broken in order to fulfill his true purpose. Human beings cannot, in Ignatius's phrase, "attain God" without going through death, the death that temporarily destroys the union of the body and soul. Vall presents several metaphors—a tree can become paper, animals can become nourishment, and grains can become flour. In a sense, all this is the "spiritualization of the material realm" (Vall, p. 146).

That Ignatius should use this imagery to refer to a sacrifice on an altar is not surprising. Sacrifices throughout almost all human religion have involved the destruction of the thing sacrificed—animals are slaughtered, their bodies immolated so that they turn into smoke. The same is done with grain offerings. Drink offerings are poured out on an altar. They are all destroyed in order to attain to a greater spiritual benefit: "Insofar as the worshiper offers not merely a surplus but the best of what he or she has to live on, the gesture of sacrifice is not merely symbolic but embodies a real act of trust and devotion" (ibid.).

Somewhat surprisingly, what Vall does not say here is what the purpose of the death and sacrifice of the Christian is— union with Christ and ultimately resurrection.

The unitive aspect of sacrifice is present for both ancient pagans and Jews. The sacrifice is placed on the altar, acted upon by the deity, and then returned back to the worshiper in a changed form so that the action of the deity would thereby be transmitted to the worshiper. That return might be through the eating of what had been sacrificed or by the sprinkling of blood on the worshiper. Thus the worshiper is also changed. And the ultimate change for the worshiper of Christ is resurrection.

With this in mind, Ignatius also tells the Magnesians, using the image of the loaf, "Therefore put aside the bad leaven, now antiquated and sour, and turn to the new leaven, which is Jesus

Christ" (*Magnesians* 10:2). Being leavened with Christ, we can become one with Him and are changed by Him.

This language that Ignatius uses of becoming "the pure bread of Christ" is striking. He identifies himself with the Eucharist. But what is the Eucharist? It is the very presence of Christ Himself among us. So if Ignatius identifies himself as the Eucharist, he identifies himself with Christ.

This identification is illustrated by a practice from the earliest years of the Church's history: the eucharistic offering was often conducted not on dedicated altars but directly on top of the tombs of the martyrs. The martyr's body is thus closely identified with the Eucharist. Even though most Divine Liturgies in our own time are not celebrated on a martyr's tomb, it is traditional for there to be relics—especially the relics of a martyr—placed inside the altar table. Such relics are also commonly sewn into the back of the antimension, the iconographic cloth that in Byzantine liturgics is opened on the altar and on which the Eucharist is conducted. Even though the altar is used for many services, the antimension is only opened for the eucharistic service.

So what we are hearing from Ignatius where he binds together his martyrdom, his own body, the Eucharist, and our Lord Jesus Christ is all expressive of some of the earliest traditions of the Church.

Let us listen to another passage from St. Paul in which he identifies himself with Christ, particularly through suffering that is joined to Christ's: "I have been crucified with Christ; it is no longer I who live, but Christ lives in me; and the *life* which I now live in the flesh I live by faith in the Son of God, who loved me and gave Himself for me" (Gal. 2:20). Paul identifies himself with Christ's sufferings by saying that he is crucified with Him. But he also says that he's no longer the one living, but Christ is living in him. His life in the flesh is now driven "by faith in the Son of God." Paul is so advanced in holiness because of his crucifixion with Christ that he says that his very life is Christ alive in him.

So we have Pauline examples of this close identification with Christ that we also see in Ignatius. The words of the Scripture shine forward all the more powerfully when we listen to those, like Ignatius, who first heard the Gospel from the apostles. It's fascinating to read Ignatius almost as a commentary on Paul or as a companion in the same theology.

Ignatius uses eucharistic language for himself when he writes to the Ephesians, "I am a sacrifice for you, consecrated for you Ephesians" (*Ephesians* 8:1b). The Eucharist is also a sacrifice, offered up on the altar of God on behalf of the people. Thus, Ignatius can say that he is a sacrifice "for you," that is, for the Ephesians. He is being offered up on God's altar both for the sake of pleasing God and also to enable the Ephesians to "live in relation to God" (*Ephesians* 8:1).

This, too, is eucharistic language. As a sacrifice, Ignatius's life is being lived "in relation to God." His true meaning and purpose are for this dedication, this sacrifice of himself for God's purposes and not his own. And since this sacrifice is made, those who partake of it likewise may "live in relation to God." Just as the Eucharist accomplishes this for us when it is offered and when we partake of it, so does Ignatius accomplish this for the Ephesians who are partaking of his sacrifice by hearing his teachings and following them. And he can accomplish this for us, as well, if we do the same.

But it is not only the sacrifice which makes Ignatius eucharistic. It is also the consecration by God. In being consecrated, he is offered up for the faithful. Literally, *consecration* is the "holy joining together," or "joining together in being made sacred," or "joining together in being set apart." Ignatius is united with God in being offered up eucharistically. And his consecration by God also consecrates those who follow him.

Ignatius also calls himself a sacrifice to God when writing to the Romans: "Pray to Christ for me that through these means [i.e., martyrdom] I may be found a sacrifice to God" (*Romans* 4:2). He is not merely being offered, but offered to God. The same is true for the Eucharist, which is offered to God and then returned to us, having been consecrated by Him, to transmit to us the divine presence.

The word Ignatius uses for "sacrifice," the Greek *thysia*, is used in pagan Greek culture for the sacrifices offered up on the altars of the pagan gods. But *thysia* is also used in the Greek Old Testament, the Septuagint, to refer to the sacrifices commanded of the Jews by God in the Torah. Ignatius's sacrificial imagery here and elsewhere "skillfully blends [both] biblical and pagan motifs" (Vall, p. 83). He intends to invoke both the Jewish inheritance of sacrifice under the Old Covenant and also the experience that his pagan or formerly pagan listeners would have had in their own temples. Christ is the fulfillment of both, and Ignatius, identifying with Christ and with the Eucharist, is a participant in that fulfillment.

THE EUCHARIST AS COMMUNION: "YOU ARE ... CHRIST-BEARERS"

If Ignatius regards the spiritual life as inextricably bound up in both fleshly and spiritual realities, and if he sees himself and others identified with Christ in eucharistic terms, then it is because of what the Eucharist is. It is communion with God, union with Him. It is the fountain of immortality.

Ignatius has a goodly number of things to say about the Eucharist as the Eucharist—that is, in terms of the actual eating and drinking of the Body and Blood of Christ in the liturgical celebration. First, it is "the bread of God," as he says to the Ephesians (*Ephesians* 5:2), situated within the prayer of the bishop and the whole church together. Within the context of that prayer, when believers commune, they are receiving nothing other than God Himself as they commune. For if that bread is Christ's Body, and if Christ is God, then Christians truly eat God when they eat "the bread of God."

Ignatius stresses that the bread is only available there in that ecclesial context: "unless a man is within the sanctuary, he lacks the bread of God" (ibid.). If anyone is outside the one sanctuary of the Church, he lacks this bread. He says that anyone who thinks he can have it outside that sanctuary deceives himself. The Eucharist is an ecclesial event, not a private act of spiritual experience. That is why it has to be offered within the prayer "of the bishop and of the whole church" (ibid.).

We might ask here what Ignatius can mean by "the whole church." He is surely aware that there are other bishops in the Church universal besides himself, so it's clear that he means the whole of the local church gathered around its own bishop.

The Eucharist is precisely a *local* event that occurs in a concrete gathering led by the local bishop.

There is also no doctrine here of sacraments that exist outside the communion of the Church, nor is the priesthood of all believers invoked so that the Eucharist may be celebrated by any layman. Ignatius says that "a valid Eucharist is to be defined as one celebrated by the bishop or by a representative of his" (*Smyrnaeans* 8:1). There is order here. The Eucharist is not "a valid Eucharist" just because someone feels in his heart that he has a right to celebrate it. Anything that is apart from the bishop is outside that one sanctuary.

But being outside the sanctuary has real effects. As Ignatius says to the Trallians, "He who is within the sanctuary is pure; he who is outside the sanctuary is not pure" (*Trallians* 7:2a). Those who are outside that one sanctuary not only lack "the bread of God," but that lack renders them "not pure." They cannot be purified apart from the one communion of the Church. Ignatius then fleshes out what he means by being "outside the sanctuary": "that is, whoever does anything apart from the bishop and the presbytery and the deacons is not pure in conscience" (*Trallians* 7:2b). Disobedience and disunity are sins against the Eucharist and render impure the consciences of those who engage in them.

Ignatius likewise writes to the Magnesians, "All of you must run together as to one temple of God, as to one sanctuary, to one Jesus Christ" (*Magnesians* 7:2). Again, notice the oneness in worship, the oneness together—this is communion. Unity in worship is part of what the Eucharist is, because there is one Jesus Christ. In Him is the unity in the temple, in the sanctuary, and therefore in the Eucharist. He says something quite similar to the Philadelphians:

> Be eager, therefore, to use one Eucharist—for there is one flesh of our Lord Jesus Christ and one cup for union with his blood, one sanctuary, as there is one bishop, together with the presbytery and the deacons my fellow slaves—so that whatever you do, you do it in relation to God. (4:2)

This oneness is not only to keep order in the Church, but it is because the Eucharist is precisely for communion. To "commune" means to come together as one, to be together in union. There can be no coming together without this oneness, and the oneness is because of the oneness of Christ Himself.

The idea that there can be communion without oneness in all things—in doctrine, in episcopacy, in spiritual life, in the bread and the cup of the Eucharist—is absent in Ignatius's letters. By this oneness in all these things, "whatever you do, you do it in relation to God." For Ignatius, Christian life cannot be determined according to the tastes and preferences of individual Christians. You don't get to decide for yourself what to believe, how to live, etc.

Indeed, the docetists illustrate this question for him: "They abstain from Eucharist and prayer because they do not acknowledge that the Eucharist is the flesh of our Savior Jesus Christ which suffered for our sins, which the Father raised up by his goodness. Those who deny God's gift are dying in their squabbles" (*Smyrnaeans* 7:1). Because they are not one in doctrine with the Church, they are out of communion, and since they are out of communion, they are "dying in their squabbles."

It's interesting to note here that the docetists appear to have excommunicated *themselves*, both from the Eucharist and also from the common prayers of the church—they have gone into schism. It's further interesting that even the heretics have a sense that a difference in doctrine on their part means that they don't pray and commune together with the Church. Heresy eventually *requires* schism. This point may be hard to grasp in our own day, when so many Christians regard heresy as merely a difference of opinion and schism as something that makes no sense—why can't we all just commune together no matter what we believe?

As Ignatius says to the Smyrnaeans, "Let no one deceive himself: even for heavenly beings and the glory of the angels and rulers both visible and invisible there is judgment, unless they believe in the blood of Christ; 'he who receives, let him receive'" (*Smyrnaeans* 6:1). You have to "believe in the blood of Christ," or else, even if you are a heavenly being, an angel, etc., then there will be judgment. The phrase "he who receives, let him receive" does not here mean receiving communion, but rather is about receiving the teaching about the Eucharist. Gregory Vall translates this, "Let the one who accepts, accept" (p. 42), echoing from the Gospels, "He who has ears [to hear], let him hear" (Matt. 11:15; 13:9, 43; Mark 4:9; Luke 8:8; 14:35).

But why would there be judgment? Why would they die? It is because the blood of Christ is an indication of His true humanity, which is what the docetists did not believe in. The Incarnation is critical dogma. If you don't believe in the true humanity of Christ, then you do not believe in Christ. It is also because of what the Eucharist is. Ignatius says to the Ephesians that they should be "breaking one loaf, which is the medicine of immortality, the antidote which results not in dying but in living forever" (*Ephesians* 20:2). If they are not eating of the "one loaf," the "medicine of immortality," "the antidote," then they cannot help but die.

And, ultimately, it is because of the nature of our life. We are not *naturally* immortal. We are only sustained in existence by God's energy. We know from Scripture that we will all be sustained by Him to exist forever, but *true* immortality, which is not merely existence but being fully alive, can only come by our participation in God, which includes eating the "one loaf."

Ignatius tells the Trallians, "You must take on gentleness and renew yourselves in faith, the Lord's flesh, and in love, the blood of Jesus Christ" (*Trallians* 8:1b). The Eucharist renews us in faith and in love, which Ignatius connects here with Christ's Body and Blood, respectively. How could such renewal take place if the Eucharist is merely a symbol? And how could such renewal take place if we are not actively communing in that divine food? What happens when we come together for that true Eucharist? Ignatius says, "Therefore be eager to meet more frequently for thanksgiving [*eucharistian*] and glory to God. For when you frequently come together, the powers of Satan are destroyed and his destructive force is annihilated by the concord of your faith" (*Ephesians* 13:1). In the peace so established by that communion, "all warfare among heavenly and earthly beings is abolished" (*Ephesians* 13:2). By coming to church and praying together and partaking of the Eucharist together, we do battle with and gain victory over the devil and all the powers of darkness. Cosmic warfare comes to an end.

In this communion, we become transformed, and the pleasures of this world no longer attract us. We are changed into people who can say with Ignatius,

> My desire has been crucified and in me there is no matter-loving fire; there is water living and speaking in me, saying from within me, "Come to the Father." I take no pleasure in the food of corruption or in the pleasures of this life. I desire the bread of God, which is the flesh of Jesus Christ (who was of the seed of David), and for drink I desire his blood, which is imperishable love. (*Romans* 6:2b–3)

In this communion, we become "companions on the way, God-bearers and shrine-bearers, Christ-bearers, bearers of holy things, in every respect adorned with the commandments of Jesus Christ" (*Ephesians* 9:2). What a powerful vision, that we can bear Christ within ourselves!

It is sad for me to reflect that there are so many Christians for whom the Eucharist is absent or for whom the Eucharist is only a symbol, a sign of an absent presence. And how sad it is that so many who would follow Christ are nonetheless caught up in the "strange plant" of heretical doctrine.

I do not know whether the services they celebrate with bread and wine (or grape juice) truly have the Eucharist or not, but if I had only the words of Ignatius to go by, with his strong vision of doctrinal and episcopal unity, I think he would not say that the Eucharist can be found outside the one Church.

He of course did not have the particular problem to deal with that we now have—a multiplicity of denominations with conflicting doctrines—though it is possible that there were groups in his time who claimed to have the Eucharist who really did not. Certainly, he insists that nothing is valid apart from the bishop, who is in communion with the whole Church. So we can probably conclude that Ignatius's ecclesiology would not have admitted to the reality of the Eucharist apart from that communion.

But he wasn't looking at our situation, nor even the situation of the Fathers of the centuries that followed him, who often asked questions about whether baptism in particular could exist outside the canonical boundaries of the Church. It doesn't make sense to project everything that Ignatius says to apply to situations he wasn't addressing. Could he have foreseen a Church in which even bishops would break away from the unity of the Church? Those problems were addressed by his successors in the centuries to come.

I chose the topic of the Eucharist to conclude our discussions of the theology of Ignatius the God-bearer of Antioch not only because of the great stress that he laid on the sacrament but also because it is truly a perfect completion for any good work of the Church. We come together to read his writings and to meditate for a while on his wisdom, and our own love and unity with one another is expressed finally in the eucharistic gathering. The Church is what it is in the Divine Liturgy, the eucharistic synaxis where all things are not only in order but most truly themselves. I am most myself when I stand before the altar and celebrate the holy mysteries, and we are all most ourselves when we join together in that one prayer, eat from that one loaf, and drink from that one cup.

Conclusion

As we close this brief study on St. Ignatius the God-bearer of Antioch, my hope is that we have in some measure felt a little bit closer to those beautiful days when the Gospel was new and still quite dangerous, when it challenged believers to a martyric dedication to the life in Christ. But why should we do that? Is it so that we can have a kind of historical nostalgia or an exercise in imagination? Or is there something more here for us?

The witness of someone like Ignatius, just like that of the apostles, is especially needed in our time because we find ourselves in a situation very much like theirs. If Christendom is still near to us at all, it is really only the *ruins* of Christendom. Christendom fell long ago. I do not think we are even in a "post-Christian" time now. More and more, the world is hostile to Christ and does not assume even basic Christian ethics, which are the historical basis for recognizing the inherent worth of every human person. We are now in a "pre-Christian" time, a time such as the one Ignatius lived in, when Christians do not live in Christian societies. But there is so much possibility of addressing the people of our time in new, creative ways that make sense to them, just as Ignatius creatively spoke to his own time.

I often meet young people these days who do not know the basic Christian message, the Gospel. On the one hand, that might seem to be cause for dismay—why did no one ever teach them? But when I meet someone like that, I do not see primarily the neglect of generations of Christians to catechize but rather someone who is not burnt out on any particular image of Christianity. Here is someone who can hear the Gospel in a fresh way, someone for whom the good news is truly good news, who will now hear it for the first time, who will hear it as new.

The message of Ignatius to Christians in a pagan world is a message we need to hear as new once again. Unlike him we do not live in a pagan world, which at least understood something about sacrifice and what it means to be human, but in a secularized one, which abhors sacrifice and degrades the human. So our task in some ways is more difficult than his.

But in other ways, the task is really the same. Like Ignatius, we live in a world cross-pressured by multiple religious ideas. Like Ignatius, we face an empire built on exploitation and warfare, both against foreign enemies and against even our own children, especially those in the womb. Like Ignatius, we face a world that does not recognize the manifestation of God in the flesh. Like Ignatius, we face a world in which it is easy to compromise our Christianity with reductions in doctrine and distortions of Christian identity. And like Ignatius, we have the apostolic faith given by Christ and the Eucharist given by Christ to strengthen us in courage, in unity, and in love.

Ignatius is valuable to us as we bear witness to a world that does not know Christ. But he is also valuable to us as we bear witness to the apostolic faith to other Christians who may feel lost in this world, especially those whose churches have changed out from under them, sometimes in ways that make them almost unrecognizable as Christian churches. We can use Ignatius's letters as a witness to the spirit and character of the early Church. And as Christians listen together to his voice, we can discover that same voice in the Orthodox Church of today.

But the Orthodox have to listen to his voice, as well! We cannot witness the fullness of Christ to non-Christians and non-Orthodox Christians if we do not listen to the voice of people like Ignatius, who bear God within themselves and show us the way to do the same. Ignatius's witness is useful not only for evangelistic purposes but for the salvation of those who are already part of the Orthodox Church and are not living up to its faith.

My hope here is that the challenge of this holy God-bearer is not something we hear and then say to ourselves, "Oh, if only people cared that much about the Gospel these days!" Some people still do. And if we are not among them, we can become those people. We can become people who say with Ignatius, "I am the wheat of God," offering ourselves up to be ground by suffering and leavened by Christ to become the "pure bread of God."

Are we ready to begin that journey with him? What would we do if we were confronted by those lions? What do we do when confronted with the strange plants of the heresies of this world? What do we do when we are tempted to compromise our faith? When confronted with all those fears and temptations, we can take courage from his words: "It is better for me to die for Jesus Christ, than to be king over the ends of the earth. I seek him who died for us; I want him who rose for us" (*Romans* 6:1).

May we drink deeply from the cup that Ignatius himself drank of, so that we, too, may be for the world a fresh and powerful witness to the Gospel of Jesus Christ.

About the Author

The V. Rev. Archpriest Andrew Stephen Damick is Chief Content Officer of Ancient Faith Ministries, former pastor (2009-2020) of St. Paul Orthodox Church of Emmaus, Pennsylvania, author of multiple books from Ancient Faith Publishing, host of several Ancient Faith Radio podcasts, and writes at Ancient Faith Blogs. He is a frequent speaker at lectures and retreats both in parishes and in other settings. He resides in Emmaus with his wife, Kh. Nicole, and their children.

ALSO BY

Andrew Stephen Damick

AN INTRODUCTION TO GOD: ENCOUNTERING THE DIVINE IN ORTHODOX CHRISTIANITY

Speaking to non-believers and believers alike, Fr. Andrew Stephen Damick attempts to create a sacred space in which we can encounter God. In this compact volume, he distills the essence of the traditional Christian faith, addressing the fundamental mysteries of where God is, who God is, why we go to church, and why Christian morality matters. If you've only heard about the Protestant or Roman Catholic version of Christianity, what he has to say may surprise you—and make you long to encounter God in Jesus Christ.

ORTHODOXY AND HETERODOXY: FINDING THE WAY TO CHRIST IN A COMPLICATED RELIGIOUS LANDSCAPE

Fr. Andrew Stephen Damick covers the gamut of ancient heresies, modern Christian denominations, fringe groups, and major world religions, highlighting the main points of each faith. This book is an invaluable reference for anyone who wants to understand the faiths of those they come in contact with—as well as their own.

Ancient Faith Publishing hopes you have enjoyed and benefited from this book. The proceeds from the sales of our books only partially cover the costs of operating our nonprofit ministry—which includes both the work of **Ancient Faith Publishing** and the work of **Ancient Faith Radio.** Your financial support makes it possible to continue this ministry both in print and online. Donations are tax-deductible and can be made at **www.ancientfaith.com.**

To view our other publications,
please visit our website: **store.ancientfaith.com**

ANCIENT FAITH RADIO

Bringing you Orthodox Christian music, readings, prayers, teaching, and podcasts 24 hours a day since 2004 at
www.ancientfaith.com